The Woman's Circle of Harmony

Removing Barriers.
Reaching your Harmony.
Recognising Life's Purpose.

Dr. Vassilia Orfanou

Absolute Author
Publishing House

Contact the Author

www.ludci.eu
vassilia@ludci.eu

Publisher: Absolute Author Publishing House
Publisher Editor: Dr. Melissa Caudle
Editor: Ruby Karyo

Paperback ISBN: 978-1-64953-006-6
Hardback ISBN: 978-1-64953-909-0
eBook ISBN: 978-1-64953-895-6

"I am a woman in the process, I'm just trying like everybody else. I try to take every conflict, every experience, and learn from it. Life is never dull."
Oprah Winfrey

TABLE OF CONTENTS

The Gate to Your Inner Voice

Abstract

How many detours must we take to find the right path? How many challenges must we endure to reach our full potential? Are setbacks and failures the only way to discover our true calling? Is it through finding a single purpose, embarking on a journey, or exploring multiple directions that we come closer to a meaningful and fulfilling life, adapting it to our unique path and blueprint?

As Aristotle once said, "Excellence is never an accident. It is always the result of high intention, sincere effort, and intelligent execution; it represents the wise choice of many alternatives - choice, not chance, determines your destiny." Striving for excellence requires intentional action and making informed decisions that shape our future.

Does the pursuit of excellence involve engaging with others, or does it lead to our downfall, hitting rock bottom before rising stronger? The reality lies somewhere in between. Personally, I believe that a person's character and qualities contribute to their essence. In contrast, their intellect and mindset can either build or destroy others. The dynamics of love and relationships are complex, captivating, and liberating. Still, indeed, one often encounters a few disappointments before finding their perfect match.

In truth, we don't exactly know what happened to Cinderella after her union with Prince Charming. Nevertheless, I choose to remain optimistic, hoping that he didn't turn out to be a complete disappointment. Undoubtedly, there are good men out there, but the question remains: where does one go to find them?

Shifting our focus to careers, many of us have dedicated countless hours, day after day, tirelessly chasing success like a never-ending race with no discernible beginning or end. We have had to navigate difficult bosses and incompatible teams while wearing a smile and getting the job done. The worst part is that years pass by, jobs change, bosses change, and teams vary, but we're left with the same bitter taste, always yearning for something better. However, every trial and tribulation endured in the professional realm brings us closer to discovering our true selves. Testing our limits, venturing into uncharted territory, and shedding anything that no longer serves us are all steppingstones toward personal growth.

The renowned Indian activist Mahatma Gandhi said, "Satisfaction lies in the effort, not in the attainment." Still, I often find myself pondering whether our efforts truly lead to tangible outcomes or if we are merely trapped in an endless cycle, where others simply take advantage of our efforts to stay ahead. This unanswered question lingers in my mind, leaving me in a state of contemplation.

Most recently, I realised that the journey itself holds significance, and denying oneself the small pleasures in life until reaching the ultimate destination is not really viable. Enjoying simple pleasures like savoring a cup of coffee on the porch, reading the newspaper, gazing out the window, immersing oneself in a favorite book, snuggling on the couch, going out for late-night drinks, welcoming new people into one's life, and prioritizing the essentials, such as eating, drinking, and sleeping well are all part of this journey.

In particular, the nightly ritual of surrendering to sleep holds undeniable importance. As Benjamin Franklin famously stated, "Early to bed and early to rise makes a man healthy, wealthy, and wise." Prioritizing a good night's sleep contributes to overall well-being, success, and wisdom.

During the sleeping hours, we bid farewell to the ceaseless chatter of our minds and tame our racing thoughts. In fact, sleep is often neglected and ruthlessly overtaken by clutches of anxiety, fear, and stress, genuinely robbing us of its precious healing hours.

It is during our sleep that we delve into meditation from within. The genuine reflection of our innermost essence resonates with our elevated existence, occasionally obscuring our self-affection and self-connection.

During that time, we can ultimately look at ourselves in the mirror and say, "I am sorry; I love you and promise to take care of you as deserved."

After a good night's sleep, when you truly feel invigorated and healed, you can recap your thoughts of not reaching your destiny's calling. And the questions remain:

Where is that bloody harmony I've been longing for so long? Where is that career path that I have always been destined for? Where is the man that will finally open his arms for me and never let me go? Would I ever feel content, relaxed, calm, and thoroughly enjoy myself in the present? Will I ever go to bed truly holding on to myself, feeling content and sleeping well, without 'that endless chatter' eating my brain alive and taking the best of me?

Chapter 1

The Awakening

One disaster after the next - a never-ending cycle of beginnings and endings in different countries, jobs, and partners. I feel tired, drained, overwhelmed, and constantly doubting myself. "When will that day come when I feel complete one way or another? Where lies my long-awaited, overdue Ithaca? A personal, safe, and incontestable earth haven – my vast and expansive island, where my existence transcends and radiates vitality and boundless optimism?"

As life unfolds daily, I find myself merely an observer in my theater of existence, where I hold the role of the sole protagonist. It's as if I have been cast to play diverse roles in scenes I have never consciously chosen, drifting further away from embracing the fullness of life and growing distant from the 'real me.' I aspire to step into the spotlight and seize the opportunities that align with my deepest desires and values. Through this intentional journey, I hope to rediscover the true essence of my existence and draw closer to the things that I hold dear to my heart.

In total dismay and utter confusion, I say one thing, but it's precisely the opposite. Could it be that other women also find themselves in the same quest for something in my cognizance?

The very contemplation of that question stirs painful irritation within me. Everything I do eventually crashes and burns, finally dissolving into an unending void. Yet, amidst the expanding emptiness, a peculiar wisdom takes root within me.

I recall Michael Novak's wise words, *The Experience of Nothingness*, "I need not to be afraid of the void. The void is part of my person. I need to enter consciously into it. To try to escape from it is to try to live a lie. It is also to cease to be. My acceptance of despair and emptiness constitutes my being; to have the courage to accept despair is to be."

And while I realise the truth behind these words, I keep pondering, "Where is the harmony and symphony to the beat of the melody I love most?

When will I stumble upon that gateway to my inner voice, where a resounding proclamation of contentment and happiness awaits? A place where

I wake up with a smile, where everything falls into place, and the universe weaves its intricate tapestry of meaning.

In my relentless quest to rediscover my lost voice, my true essence, I embark on the journey of writing this book. It becomes a delicate balancing act as I find myself and extend a helping hand to other women who seek to regain or unearth their own voices. Perhaps, in guiding others, I will ultimately find my own voice.

Through the turbulence of my inner struggles, I have recognized the futility of allowing fellow women to tread the same arduous path. Why waste precious time when I can guide them toward unraveling the authentic sources of their happiness? In empowering others, I may uncover the profound wisdom and clarity I seek for myself.

As I continue this journey, I must admit that I'm still stumbling through a steep learning curve. Exploring other women's lenses, perspectives, and ideas sometimes feels like a rollercoaster ride, where my mind gets ignited or bombed with unexpected revelations, leaving me questioning the validity of my thoughts.

It's like attending a wild intellectual circus, where ideas perform acrobatics and dive through flaming hoops. My mind desperately tries to keep up with the spectacle. I laugh at the absurdity of it all, realizing that even the most well-formed thoughts can take unexpected detours and somersault into a sea of uncertainty.

Amidst the comedy of it, there's a hidden treasure: the affirmation that my thoughts, however imperfect or unconventional, have their own validity. In this collision of perspectives, where my mind gets stretched, tickled, and occasionally blown to bits, I realize the importance of embracing the beautiful chaos of intellectual exploration.

Writing about my present reminds me of where it all began, the harsh experiences, and my intention to never revisit those dark moments that keep tormenting me, but will never really get the best of me… I know that much…and you know it too…

Finally awakened from my thirty-something Rapunzel years of poor sleep, my sole desire remains to press the restart button, rewinding my past experiences to understand where I am going next.

As I ponder, I stumble upon a profound realization that feels like finding a hidden stash of chocolate in the back of your cupboards. I wholeheartedly embrace this emerging version of myself, like a caterpillar finally transforming into a fabulous butterfly.

It's like I've unlocked a secret level in the game of life, where the power-ups and upgrades are all about embracing my quirks and imperfections. I've become the CEO of my life.

Gone are the days of trying to fit into a mold never designed for me. Now, I'm strutting down my newfound path with all the grace and confidence of a penguin in stilettos. It's liberating – like walking for hours, throwing away your uncomfortable shoes, and slipping into fuzzy slippers.

So, here's to embracing the chaos, the messiness, and the glorious imperfections. Cheers to becoming the woman I was always meant to be and embracing the adventure of this crazy journey called life.

It is now or never the time to buckle up and enjoy the ride of a lifetime! And by "lifetime," I mean the glorious span of years I have left before I transform into a mystical dust fairy. Yep, you heard that right; I'm planning for a career change in the afterlife.

But hey, while I'm still rocking this mortal coil, I'm determined to squeeze every drop of joy, adventure, and laughter out of it. I will embrace the twists and turns, the ups and downs, like a rollercoaster junkie on a sugar rush. Life's too short to sweat the small stuff – after all, I'll be dusting up the fairy realm soon enough!

So, let's sprinkle some magic on this journey, my lady friends. Let's dance in the rain, chase rainbows, and make memories that would make even the dust bunnies jealous. I'll be the quirkiest dust fairy they've ever seen, with a trail of laughter and glitter wherever I go.

So, join me in savoring every moment because who knows what awaits us beyond this fantastical ride. Whether it's soaring through the skies or tripping over our own feet, let's make this journey one for the storybooks. Cheers to embracing life until we become the stuff of legends – or at least dust fairies with attitude!

Oh, let me tell you, I may not have all the answers, but I'm strapping on my bravery-red *Alice in Wonderland* boots and venturing forth into the wild world once again. It's like being a novice tightrope walker without a safety net, but who needs a net when you've got an abundance of hope?

I eagerly await that glorious moment when I gaze into the mirror, wrinkles, and all, and confidently whisper, "You made it, girl! You conquered it all, kid!" Cue the confetti cannons and a chorus of applause because that will be the sweetest victory dance of my life.

Here's the thing, my friend, no matter how many years go by, I'll always have that mischievous spark of a kid inside me. You know, the one who still secretly wants to jump in puddles, believes in magic, and laughs at awful puns. Embracing that inner child is my biggest success. I plan to hold on to it tighter than a toddler clutching their favorite teddy bear.

So, as I navigate this crazy world, I'll wear my hopeful heart on my sleeve and continue to embrace the wonder and joy that comes with being forever young at heart. Life may throw curveballs, but I'll be here, cheering myself on and reminding me, "You made it, kid! And you'll keep making it, one adventure at a time." Cheers to remaining forever young on this wild ride we call life!

Reflecting on the good old teenage years - being noticed was like a badge of honor. But let's be honest, it wasn't exactly my sole life goal, as I was a true whisperer. I had more pressing matters to attend to, like figuring out why my lioness hair had a mind of its own every day or why my fashion choices were entirely questionable. It took me a good chunk of years to finally navigate the treacherous maze of self-discovery and get a clue about who I really was and where the heck I was headed.

It was like playing an epic *Witcher* game of hide-and-seek with my identity, and boy, was I an expert at hiding from myself and getting all the punches in the end! It's almost as if my teenage years were an elaborate disguise party, with me trying on different personalities and hobbies like they were outrageous costumes. Let's just say I could have given Marilyn Monroe and Audrey

Hepburn a run for their money in the outfit-changing department.

But hey, I stumbled upon some golden nuggets of self-realization during all the confusion and questionable life choices. Slowly but surely, like a tortoise on a caffeine boost, I discovered my passions, values, and quirky path in this crazy world.

So, here I am, older and wiser (well, maybe just older, and still wrinkle free), reflecting on those awkward teenage and early adulthood years and realizing that it's all part of the grand adventure. Life may throw us curveballs and questionable fashion trends, but the journey of self-discovery truly matters. At least now I can look back and laugh at my disasters because, let's face it, those neon colorful shirts were never a good idea.

So, cheers to the years of figuring out who we are and where we're headed, even if it takes a lifetime of questionable choices, embarrassing moments, and good laughs. Let's embrace the wild ride of self-discovery and remember that the journey is as important as the destination. And who knows, maybe one day we'll look back and proudly say, "Yep, I finally found my way... and my sense of everything!"

Delving into the somber depths of my past, I must confront the poignant truth that my upbringing was colored by the presence of a younger sister and a fiercely determined, single-minded woman who served as my unwavering pillar of strength and determination. However, the foundation upon which our family stood - crumbled into irreparable fragments when my parents made the gut-wrenching decision to part ways. I was a mere twelve years old then - innocence still clinging to my being.

As I reflect upon those bygone years, memories of my father emerge like hazy apparitions. A figure of contradictions, he possessed a kindhearted nature intertwined with a perplexing blend of sociability and antisocial tendencies. A peculiar man, we shared little in common, and a sense of detachment pervaded our interactions.

On the other hand, my mother possessed an audacious spirit, an air of cunning foxiness, and a sharp intellect that resonated with me on a deeper level. Though our interests rarely aligned, unspoken respect and more profound love gradually formed between us. After all, a mother's intuition - that profound maternal instinct, always seems to possess an uncanny wisdom. Yet, even within this complex bond, I can attest that moments of anger were not uncommon, as clashes of wills and perspectives took their toll.

Their ill-fated union, forged in the fires of arranged matrimony, catalyzed a chain of ruinous events and a cacophony of futile memories. My sister and I found ourselves stranded in the murky abyss, grappling with the overwhelming task of navigating an uncertain path forward. Lost, adrift, and burdened by an omnipresent sense of displacement, we forged ahead, holding hands and fueled by sheer determination and an unspoken resilience that we both carry today.

Amidst the remnants of shattered familial stitching, we persisted, clinging to the fragments of our shared history. Through the chaos and confusion, we discovered a resilience within ourselves that we never knew existed. We learned that sometimes the act of simply moving forward, no matter how uncertain the destination, can serve as a testament to our strength, motivation, genuine spirit, and resilience.

And so, we carried on, writing our own narrative amidst the remnants of the one that had unraveled. Forged by hardship, our journey unfolded, an unwritten tale awaiting its climax, where, perhaps, a glimmer of hope may yet emerge from the shadows of our past.

Our parents' failed union molded our being… shaped our essence, and perhaps composed the unique song of our lives. "Every heart sings a song incomplete until another heart whispers back. Those who wish to sing always find a song. At the touch of a lover, everyone becomes a poet," Plato quotes.

Now, I must admit, I'm not exactly sure if I possess the vocal prowess of a pop diva, the lyrical finesse of a renowned poet, or the writing skills of a literary genius. But hey, what I lack in traditional talent, I more than make up for in my ability to ignite a wide range of irresistible passions. And let me tell you, those passions can be a wild mix of good and bad.

On the one hand, I can captivate hearts with my charm and charisma, leaving a trail of swooning admirers in my wake. They can't resist the magnetic pull of my irresistible allure. It's like I have a secret superpower, and I'm not afraid to use it to spread a little joy and mischief.

Let's not overlook the fact that I can also rouse some not-so-positive passions. Like accidentally setting off a small firework in a crowded room, my presence can sometimes ignite a storm of drama and chaos. It's a talent, really. Everyone's calm and collected one moment, and the next, there's pandemonium like a circus tent on fire. *Oops, I did it again* – as the one and only Britney sings!

So, while I may not have the conventional talents of a singer, poet, or writer, I'll gladly embrace my knack for stirring up passions, for better or worse. Life is never dull when I'm around, and I've come to accept that it's all part of my quirky charm. So, buckle up, my friends, because, with me, you're in for a rollercoaster ride of irresistible passions, where laughter, chaos, and a dash of trouble are always on the menu. Let the wild and unpredictable adventure begin! For sure, authentic and memorable.

As my mother always tells me, she has had two blessings in life: My sister and I. And then she cries and talks on her own - like an old gramophone playing the same old songs without stopping, even if you unplug it or throw it out of the window. It rings in my ears repeatedly - in my sleep, while running, watching TV, or listening to the radio. A never-ending Chihuahua that I must love, but also makes me angry at every chance it gets…

So, going back to the chaotic symphony of my parents' tumultuous relationship, there was no shortage of drama, fiery arguments, and enough tension to rival a Hollywood blockbuster. It was a never-ending rollercoaster ride with countless fights that could've given professional wrestlers a run for their money. I swear, their arguments had the power to shake the very foundations of our humble abode.

The intensity of their clashes instilled a deep-rooted fear within me, as if I was living in a war zone where explosions of anger were the norm. I would tiptoe around the house, desperately trying to avoid triggering another battle between them. It became a daily survival mission, navigating through the treacherous emotional minefield that our home had become.

But amidst the chaos and fear, a peculiar longing began to take hold of me. I yearned for love beyond the thunderous arguments and the bitter resentments that seemed to consume my parents. I craved a profound, so sacrificial love that it could only exist in the realm of epic romances or Greek tragedies.

I wanted the kind of love that would make Romeo and Juliet's passion seem like a mere summer fling. The type of love where one would willingly lay down their life for the other, even if it meant dramatically uttering poetic last words while dramatically clutching at their heart. Okay, maybe not that dramatic, but you get the picture.

This insatiable desire for all-encompassing love led me to make some questionable relationship choices. I abandoned partners left and right, like a skilled escape artist, because they could never offer me that grandiose, self-sacrificial love I yearned for. Poor souls, they didn't stand a chance in the face of my impossible romantic standards.

Looking back, it's a hilarious and somewhat tragic pattern. My parents' explosive relationship moulded me into a hopeless romantic with a penchant for over-the-top theatrics. At least it makes for an interesting story to tell at dinner parties, right?

So, there you have it, the tale of a fear-stricken soul who dared to dream of a love so epic it could rival any Shakespearean play. It might not be the most conventional desire, but who said love couldn't be slightly dramatic, spicy, and downright entertaining?

For real, realizing and accepting my parents' love-hate relationship pushing me to the precipice of internal conflict, and in response, I chose to simply fade away. Engaging in physical or emotional battles has never been my forte. No matter how hard I strive, my glass inevitably fills to the brim, only to be spilled over, perpetuating my self-fulfilling prophecy that nothing lasts forever.

Going back to my parents, they were never meant to be aside from bringing us into this futile world and trying to make my existence matter, some way, somehow. The thought of them staying together was impossible to comprehend. Why did they even stay together for so long?

"What were they holding on to? Despite trying to determine the facts, nothing made sense to me at the time. Compromise was the only thing that came to mind…Staying put till their kids grow."

Observing them, I could see my mother's unhappiness, despite not showing her weaknesses or vulnerabilities. Looking back, her strength and encouragement got us by, and the same stubbornness that shaped our character and made us who we are today. One thing is real-you either love or hate us. For sure, both my sister and I have the unique capability to make anyone crazy and longing for more…

Amidst the divorce's chaos and aftermath, my mother packed our belongings into our white sports car and whisked us away to the seaside. At that moment, the journey felt like a fairy tale, as if a gallant prince had arrived on his majestic white horse to rescue us. However, the bitter truth was the prince never indeed came. My mother envisioned a better upbringing for her children, far away from the toxicity surrounding us. With determination in her heart and no financial security, she defied all odds. She made it happen, shouldering the burdens and challenges that came her way while caring for two children.

Today, I stand in awe and pay my utmost respect for her. She was a true, over-the-top lady badass who triumphed over adversity and raised two remarkable ladies in the process.

Not sure where she found that courage and strength, though. Looking at things from where I currently stand, she was driven by her motherly instincts. And she was right to think that growing up in a new surrounding would better our health, spirit, and mental growth. We had already seen a lot during those trying times, way too early. These times would make us or break us forever more!

Raising us by the beach was her way of letting us be children and not grow up way too fast. Truth be told, we grew up too fast, anyway. We had to. One slap after the other. Sadly enough, our destinies did not involve growing up as normal children or even teenagers. We simply had to grow up fast.

Relocating to the new house ushered in a distinct vibration and energy, brimming with a luminosity that seemed to embrace both the heavens and the endless expanse of the sea. Every corner exuded coziness, an airy ambiance that danced with life itself.

What I remember the most was the secret haven atop our house-a little slice of paradise – our terrace - a celestial haven atop our house held the key to a slice of paradise. It painted a world of wonder with the open sky and sea as its canvas. There, time dissolved, and I lost myself in the dance of clouds, the symphony of seagulls, and the serenade of crashing waves. It became our muse, where dreams took flight and the boundless aspirations of my soul found solace. The terrace, a shimmering testament to the eternal union of sky and sea, is forever etched in my memories.

Time became a mere illusion on the terrace, for it bowed to the enchantment of the vista. I would lose myself in the dance of clouds, their graceful pirouettes painting ephemeral portraits against the canvas of the heavens. The sun, a resplendent maestro, would conduct the symphony of daylight, casting its golden hues upon the world below. The moon, a luminous poet, would pen verses of silver upon the obsidian sky.

We would stand there, entranced, as nature's verses unfolded before us, their lyrical beauty intertwining with the fibers of our being.

In those moments, we would find solace, a respite from the cacophony of life's demands. We would become cynical poets of the time-lapse senses, drinking in the celestial hues, savoring the salty tang of the sea-kissed air, and etching the whispers of the wind into the corridors of our pure but sorrowful hearts.

The terrace became our sanctuary, where dreams took flight on the wings of imagination. There, we felt closest to the ethereal wonders of the universe, where the vastness of the sky mirrored the boundless aspirations that danced within our ethereal souls.

And now, as I gaze back upon my memories, it is the terrace that shimmers brightest—a testament to the eternal union of sky and sea, a testament to the indomitable spirit that soared upon its sacred stage, and of course, our endless BS!

My mischievous sister, Electra, and I often conspired to play truant from school, using the terrace as our clandestine hideout. It was our sanctuary, where we and our buddies would escape the clutches of education and dive headfirst into hours of spirited conversation.

Oh, the discussions we had! We covered every topic under the sun and the moon till we could not figure out the day from the night and opposite, discussing the meaning of life with the latest celebrity gossip. There was no subject too trivial or profound for our curious minds. We would debate, argue, and passionately defend our viewpoints and opinionated remarks, as if we were scholars engaging in an intellectual duet. If only our teachers knew how we would avoid a math class!

When our thirst for knowledge was temporarily quenched, we summoned more friends to join the terrace party. It was a motley crew of eccentrics, gathering like a flock of seagulls to share in our nonsensical banter. We engaged in verbal acrobatics, exchanging witty remarks and clever comebacks with the finesse of seasoned comedians.

Snacking and drinking were essential components of our terrace adventures. We had a stash of snacks that could rival a supermarket aisle, and we indulged in them with reckless abandon. Our laughter would echo through the air as we devoured chips, cookies, and sugary treats. We were the masters of our snack-filled universe, ruling over our kingdom of empty chip bags and soda cans.

Oh, how our mother remained blissfully unaware of our covert operations on the terrace! If only they knew the hours we spent out there, avoiding academia and embracing the joy of nonsense. It was our little rebellion, our secret uprising against the monotony of school and the responsibilities of adulthood looming on the horizon.

So, there you have it-the tale of the terrace escapades, where skipping school transformed into a grand adventure of intellectual sparring, silly conversations, and an endless supply of snacks. It was a refuge from the ordinary, a place where time stood still, and laughter echoed in the wind. And as we sipped our sodas and munched on our snacks, we felt like the kings and queens of our own little nonsensical kingdom.

Of course, my mother, Athena, preferred we invited our friends over and knew everything about the terrace. Still, she always gave us the third degree, anyway. Little did I know it was her way of keeping us closer a while longer, watching us like a hawk and ensuring we were well-behaved. Now I have come to my senses; the terrace was her subliminal idea!

And so, time passed, and we embarked on our growth journey. At a time that I cannot exactly recall, our grandparents gracefully joined our household by the beach, extending their support to my hardworking mother, who often traveled extensively to provide for us. Their presence became a pillar of strength, joy, warmth, and fun times, ensuring we could relax and be foolish without regrets.

I particularly enjoyed, loved, and cherished every time I spent with both. But I used to spend a lot of time with my grandpa, Aristotle. He was one of the few people I respected, loved dearly, and truly thought of the world of him. I looked up to him as a strong, dedicated, and loving grandpa who taught me most of the things I know today, and misses him even these days. He may have been strict but his approach in life was scolded by my grandma, a relatively simple woman but lively, warm, and wise. They stayed together for 45 years till death eventually separated them.

Despite their contrasting personalities, their union remains an extraordinary testament to a successful partnership. Undoubtedly, my grandmother steered the ship and made it flourish. She did that with charm, wittiness, Italian flair, and cooking! I can still vividly recall how they would gaze into each other's eyes, standing by each other's side through thick and thin, bound in a commitment to weather life's storms.

Their relationship had a very positive impact on us. Stepping into our house at the time meant stepping into a familiar scent of roses, basil, freshly baked cookies, and delectable cakes. Grandma Eftyhia possessed unparalleled culinary prowess – she was indeed the finest cook. Revisiting those cherished memories, from time to time, I can still savor the flavors of her dishes and recall the comforting warmth of her hand on my face or the bliss of slumbering on her lap. Oh, how those were truly happy days!

Unfortunately for us, our weekdays were packed with school, reading, sports, and arts. Between our lives in Greece, Italy, the US, and the rest of the World, we also travelled back and forth for school and summer camp in the USA.

When it comes to my 'Dad memories' – to this date, I have very limited memories - he was rather absent most of my teenage and adult years. I recall the time that he bought us our first dog, Beauty, and our first giant Christmas tree, but equally so when our dog bit a huge chank of his arm trying to protect me. I also vividly remember my parents' fights, with my father yelling and throwing objects everywhere. I rushed to pick up my sister and lock us in our room, putting the music loud and joking around so that she would be ruined less than I.

As the turbulent chapters of our family's story unfolded, my mother, like a brave heroine, uncovered a painful truth: my father's anger often spilled onto me, caught in the crossfire of their never-ending quarrels. A heart-wrenching realization left us reeling in a tempest of emotions. With a heavy heart, my mother mustered the strength to confront us, her children, seeking our permission to break free from the chains that bound her to our tumultuous household. The weight of her words hung in the air, thick with a mixture of sorrow and hope.

We, too, carried the scars of their battles etched upon our souls. The fear that had gripped us for far too long now mingled with a bittersweet yearning for a life untainted by aggression and discord. In that poignant moment, we found our voices and answered her plea with a resounding affirmation.

And so, with a mixture of trepidation and newfound liberation, we severed the ties that held us to our father's stormy presence. We embarked on a journey into the unknown, stepping away from the wreckage of our past and into a future tinged with apprehension and hope.

It was a decision wrapped in sorrow and bravery, for we had to bid farewell to the fragments of a family that once was, accepting the bitter truth that some wounds could only heal in the absence of what caused them. The echoes of our footsteps reverberated through the hallways, carrying both the weight of sorrow and the promise of a brighter tomorrow.

As we left him behind, our hearts carried the burden of shattered dreams and unfulfilled promises. Yet, in that poignant departure, we embraced the flickering embers of resilience. We welcomed the opportunity to rebuild, to forge a new path that would be defined not by conflict, but by the pursuit of peace and healing.

It was a painful farewell that kindled the flames of hope within us. Together, we ventured forth, hand in hand, determined to break free from the shadows of our past and find solace in the arms of a future yet unwritten and quite uncertain.

Our hard times did not stop there. Seeing my poor mother struggle to make ends meet made me sick to my stomach, especially when she had to do it all alone. We tried to help as much as possible - given the means available. I have been suffering from stomach ulcers and ulcerative colitis since my early youth. All I remember were stress, anxiety, limited food, working and studying hard, and no outings or parties with friends. We grew up the hard way, for sure. Considering the turmoil, we turned out okay…

In the early days, we transformed the basement of our humble abode into a dazzling fashion gallery, where dreams shimmered like sequins and creativity knew no bounds. As our ambitions soared, we sought a larger canvas to paint our vision upon. So, we boldly embarked on a quest, renting another house to birth our dreams anew. And now, here we stand, in the bustling streets of Athens, where our current business thrives, a testament to the unwavering spirit that courses through our veins.

Amidst the whirlwind of success, there is a figure, a force of nature, who has given her all for us. My mother, a woman of indomitable strength and unwavering dedication, has never known the luxury of relaxation, the simple pleasure of a leisurely meal, or the tranquil embrace of restful slumber. She is a ceaseless whirlwind, fueled by a resolute will and an unwavering love for her family.

Her sacrifice has shaped me, sculpting me into a fearless warrior, stubborn in the face of adversity and determined to conquer the odds. Her unwavering commitment has bestowed upon me the gift of strength. This unyielding resolve propels me forward even when doubt whispers in my ear.

Yet, in the depths of my being, a seed of fear takes root, nurtured by the shadow of her relentless devotion. I am left in awe of her unwavering dedication and haunted by the daunting question: Will I ever be able to live up to the monumental role of a mother?

The weight of her sacrifice bears down upon me, and I wonder if I can ever possess even a fraction of her courage, unshakable resolve, and selfless love. The fear of falling short of failing to measure up to the woman who has given her all echoes through the corridors of my heart.

Amidst this fear, I find solace in knowing she raised me to be strong, resilient, and capable. She has equipped me with the tools to face my doubts head-on, embrace the challenges, and find my own path as a mother. I may stumble and falter, but I carry within me the spirit she has instilled—an unyielding determination to rise, overcome, and create my own unique life.

So, I step forward, my heart beating with both trepidation and hope, knowing that the woman who has shown me the heights of selflessness and dedication will forever guide me through the depths of uncertainty. With her unwavering love as my guiding light, I venture forth, ready to embrace my life journey with equal parts strength and vulnerability, knowing that I possess the spirit to keep going, no matter what.

While growing up, my sister and I were simply everything she had and no other life. Still, we caused little trouble. We were good kids, down to earth, friendly, and rather kind and generous to others. Mostly, we never really caused any distress.

Electra and I helped with laundry and household chores, but it was not easy, not easy at all. Even though my mother struggled to put food on the table, she finally made ends meet and raised us to the best of her abilities, with no-one really to turn to. Determined as she was, we became the people we are today. Michelle Obama has said, "Success isn't about how much money you make; it's about the difference you make in people's lives."

My mother truly made a difference in our lives. Our life depended on her determination, discipline, and grace, which found us in a sacred, safe heaven when everything around us would only scream "Wwhat a f… disaster."

Ultimately, she made it but sacrificed her being and womanhood for our progression. I fathom this is what motherhood is all about - pure and unconditional love for your children. Giving away all that you are and all you have for your children to breathe, even if you know you may be giving your last breath.

Ah, my dear absentee father, a master of disappearing and conveniently timed vanishing acts. After the divorce, he made three appearances in our lives, as if he had checked a box on his to-do list to fulfill his obligatory fatherly duties. How commendable.

It's no wonder that Kurt Nerburn's words, dripping with bitter truth, resonate with such painful accuracy, "It is much easier to become a father than to be one." Oh, the profundity of that statement! I have witnessed firsthand the empty chasm left by a father's absence, and it has made me think twice about diving headfirst into the treacherous waters of marriage and parenthood.

Becoming a parent, my friends, is no simple feat. It's not just a matter of fulfilling a biological role; it's a commitment that requires throwing one's ego out the window, preferably with an extravagant flourish. It demands sacrifice, heartache, and a never-ending supply of tissues to wipe away the tears of frustration and disappointment.

And let's not forget the delightful possibility of parting ways with your partner, leaving you to pick up the shattered fragments of your life, much like my dear sister and I had to do. It's like a jigsaw puzzle of misery, trying to assemble the scattered pieces while navigating the minefield of emotional baggage.

The thought of subjecting my hypothetical child to such chaos and heartbreak is unbearable. No, thank you. I'll gladly steer clear of that rollercoaster ride, keeping my sanity intact and my ego safely intact—where it belongs.

So, here I stand, resolved in my decision to resist the siren song of marriage and parenthood, knowing full well the thorny path it entails. Perhaps it's a self-protective measure to shield myself from the pitfalls and pain that may lie in wait. Or maybe it's a wise choice, a testament to my unwillingness to repeat past mistakes.

Whatever the reason, I will forge my path, embracing a life where ego can roam freely, sacrifices are made willingly, and heartache is kept at bay. And if that means not becoming a parent, then so be it. After all, who needs sleepless nights, dirty diapers, and melodramatic family dynamics when I can have peace, quiet, and a fully intact sense of self?

So, cheers to all the brave souls who venture into the realms of parenthood, braving the storms and picking up the pieces along the way. I'll be over here, basking in the glory of a life free from such complexities and laying that burden on my father.

Unfortunate as it may sound, we never really forged any relationship and had nothing in common. Speaking of his death, it came in silence. Still, I never felt any sorrow or grief but anger, which grew deeper until he passed away - a couple of days before my master's graduation. It took a lot of time till I could openly and sadly say, "I am angry at you, Dad, I am angry."

His death was passed to me by my sister. With her own impeccable drama-queen style, coupled with her faultless fashion style and her hand on her head, pouring tears all over the place breaks the news like it was a disaster bequeathed upon us two - handing in his ring, looking at me with bloodshed tearful big deer eyes. "Dad knows you will never forgive him, but he wants you to have a piece of him as you are and still will be a part of him." She hugged me in tears. I hugged her back, knowing that my mission to think of him in a positive, but pitiful way was successful. I gave myself a pat on the shoulder and buried all my unexpressed feelings toward him that day. I looked at my sister and bluntly uttered, "What's wrong with you? Take it easy now – you retard!"

Two months in, my fears were unleashed with anger once more. I was furious at him for leaving my mother to make everything happen. I was glad that the universe had finally taken its natural direction. As harsh and strange as this may sound what I saw in him is exactly what I see in all men: abandonment, self-centrism, narcissism, and egotism, when I have always longed for unconditional love, sacrifice, and putting the other person first.

Before his passing, he made a few attempts to reconnect with me. Still, my stubbornness prevented me from allowing him back into my life, guarding my heart and keeping him at a distance. I believed I would be better off if I remained ignorant of his presence.

However, in recent years, I have found the strength to forgive him, understanding that I would never truly find happiness in my relationships with men without forgiveness. This realization took time to crystallize, but ultimately, it led me to embrace forgiveness as a path toward my contentment.

Still, till that moment came, for over 20 years, this bunch of side-tracked feelings turned into a total mistrust for all males later in my life.

"What was it? How did it feel to trust someone inevitably, without a doubt, change of mind, or perception?" There was no time for boys. "Like a baby cry, time collapses in the blink of an eye. He becomes a toddler, then a child, a boy, a teenager, and then a man."

During that tumultuous period, life burdened us with numerous expectations, thrusting us into adulthood prematurely, robbing us of the chance to experience a carefree childhood.

Still, amidst the weight of responsibility, fragments of our innocence were preserved, thanks mainly to our grandparents' understanding that we were still just children.

In the intricate dance of emotions, we became masters of containment, meticulously packaging our feelings into elaborate gift boxes, each a treasure trove of unspoken thoughts and suppressed emotions. But oh, in my case, it's as if I stuffed an entire Thanksgiving feast into a tiny turkey, desperately trying to contain the overflowing chaos within its seams.

And then there's my dear sister, floating through life with blissful ignorance, utterly unaware of the gritty truths that lurked just beyond her bubble of obliviousness. Oh, how her innocence deepened her obliviousness, nourishing a belief that the world was her personal concierge, ready to cater to her every whim.

It's a marvel, really, witnessing her entitlement in action. She flutters about, expecting the universe to unfold at her command as if she were the protagonist of a cosmic sitcom. I half expect her to snap fingers and summon a troupe of loyal servants to fulfill her every desire. Ah, the joys of delusion!

Meanwhile, I navigate the treacherous territory of my overstuffed turkey of emotions, tiptoeing around the imminent explosion that threatens to burst forth at any moment. Oh, the absurdity of it all! I am a walking pressure cooker, brimming with unexpressed thoughts and bottled-up frustrations, desperately needing a comedic relief valve.

But amidst the chaos and the ridiculousness, there is a flicker of understanding. We all have unique ways of coping and navigating the labyrinth of emotions that life throws our way. My turkey may be bursting at the seams, and my sister may be the oblivious queen of entitlement. Still, we are united in our flawed humanity and unquestionable gorgeousness.

So, here's to us, the masters of emotional packaging, the misfits of feeling containment. May we find humor in our quirks, release the pressure with a good laugh, and remember that even the most ornate gift boxes can't contain the messiness of the human experience.

Years later, my mindset materialized in donning a new cap, tossing aside the old one, and embarking on a fresh start. It was a solitary journey, with few genuinely understanding the depths of my being.

In the case of my sister, her mindset manifested itself as a child cradled in her arms, with a husband who bore a striking resemblance to our father (a bit nicer and present, though), with the highest probability that another child in our family will endure the same heartache we once did. It infuriates me even to contemplate the injustice of it all, as I dearly love our precious Konstanz.

Life moved much faster than we could even ponder, and we started chasing after it. We had to help our mother with work, juggle school, private tutoring, competitive sports, and secure our lives to 'independence' - a significant word brainwashed by our mother quite early in age.

That word became both a curse and our motivation. She always used to say, "Be independent" and "Never rely on anyone but yourself." If you want to turn to someone, just visit your mother. And so, it was…

We repeatedly listened to the old gramophone, aside from whether we have eaten, studied, made some friends, met anyone in our lives, etc. It is tiring to be a mother, my God!

Consciously, my sister and I adapted to the new way of accepting and dealing with inner rewards and considering what mother Athena taught us. What mattered the most was the love within and the genuineness she showed us.

Aside from independence, Athena also taught us how to be responsible and conscious of others even before we knew what those two words meant. We felt it to our core. There was no time to think! Just act. And for many years, it served my purpose.

I was good at school, university, my jobs, and initial relationships – when I was not thinking or analyzing as much.

When the mind chatter began, I suffocated, as if deprived of oxygen, until the moment of awakening. The burden of unexpressed emotions, the weight of every hurt, anguish, pain, and disappointment, remained concealed within me. I carried on with the facade of normalcy.

Reflecting on that time, I realized I was leading a dual existence. Outwardly, everything appeared perfect and under control, but inwardly, chaos reigned. Hidden emotions, like toxic substances, lurked, threatening to engulf my very being, with no clear beginning or end in sight.

The words of Martin Luther King Jr. put me at peace, "We must accept definite disappointment, but never lose infinite hope."

And that's when my dual personality emerged, casting me as its solitary target. It was a perplexing situation I found myself in, with the presence of not just one but two distinct personas inhabiting my being, one of whom remains an enigma to this day. I had unwittingly confined myself within two immaculate but separate boxes: one encompassed a driven go-getter, a relentless pursuer of goals, a dedicated student and professional; the other embodied a lovable character, cherishing moments with friends and always on the move. Frequently, these two personalities got intertwined, not knowing where I was going or doing next, leaving me naked, confused, and perplexed.

Ah, the tapestry of my younger years, woven with delicate threads of shyness, sensitivity, fear, and perpetual loneliness. Oh, how I longed to speak, to express the depths of my affection to those I held dear, especially to that eternal platonic crush who ignited a fire within my heart for over 20 years regardless of the partners and, of course, came and disappeared in thin air.

I can still vividly recall that fateful day in school, a concoction of nervous anticipation and wild courage bubbling within me. Determined to make my intentions known, I yearned to announce my desire to be with him, to reveal the secrets of my heart. But alas, fate had its own wicked sense of humor.

Instead of mustering the words, I entrusted my best friend at the time to deliver my heartfelt message. Oh, the dramatic flair! I imagined her gracefully approaching him like a messenger of love, as I eagerly awaited his response.

And then he came, seeking me out with anticipation in his eyes. But in a whirlwind of anxiety, I vanished, retreating into the sanctuary of the toilets, leaving him to search for me, bewildered and lost.

Little did I know that this chase, this dance of romantic uncertainty, would continue for years, an intricate tango of missed connections and untamed desires, not just with him, but with others that could not even match him…or so I told myself…

Oh, the naivety of youth! I thought we were caught in a grand romantic narrative, where destiny would intertwine our lives in a grand finale of love and understanding. Yet, as the years passed, reality seeped in, and we both made a conscious decision to halt the chase, to release the grip of unrequited longing.

It was a bittersweet realization, a moment where we acknowledged the futility of clinging to a love that remained forever out of reach. We bid farewell to the tantalizing dance, to the echoes of what could have been, and we embraced the uncertainty of a future untethered from the whims of unrequited affection.

And so, the chase ended, but not without leaving traces of lessons learned and hearts marked. It taught me the delicate balance between vulnerability and self-preservation, between pursuing love and accepting what is. It ignited a fire within me, a determination to seize life's joys, embrace the rollercoaster of emotions, and savor beauty in every unpredictable twist and turn.

Oh, the complexities of the human heart, forever entangled in a web of longing and surrender. Though the chase may have ended, its imprint lingers, a reminder of the passion and anxieties accompanying the pursuit of love. And as I look back upon those moments, I smile, knowing that each step, each fleeting connection, has shaped the tapestry of my womanhood, turning it into a mosaic of resilience, growth, authenticity, beauty, and an unwavering belief in the power of love.

In the tapestry of my life, another man emerged, a beacon of love and healing that illuminated the darkest corners of my soul. For a decade, he embraced me with his tenderness, kindness, and unwavering love that became the balm to my wounded heart. Oh, how he held me in his arms, refusing to let go, until the fateful moment arrived when we knew it was time to release our grasp.

I envisioned marrying this extraordinary man, his beauty, kindness, and sweetness weaving a tapestry of love that enveloped me. But amidst the depths of affection, I was suffocating, trapped within the confines of that all-consuming love. I yearned to see more and experience life beyond our relationship's narrow lens. It wasn't about finding solace in the arms of another man; it was about seeking the vastness of existence that beckoned me.

Desperate to maintain a connection, we embarked on a tumultuous journey of friendship, a rollercoaster ride of back-and-forth that inflicted equal pain upon us both. But deep within, I knew that this was the right decision, not only for my own growth but for his well-being. The path of separation, though agonizing, was the path that would lead us both to greater fulfillment.

I can still recall that serendipitous *rendezvous* at the bar, where I, perpetuating the pattern of enlisting friends for assistance, dispatched another companion to initiate a conversation. Oh, the brilliance of her opening line! She approached him, requesting an aspirin on my behalf. What an unexpected and amusing way to spark a connection! And there he stood, bringing the aspirin himself, seizing the opportunity to inquire about picking me up later and the precise location. That simple exchange set the stage for a decade of sheer bliss, love, and magnificence.

He became my healer, mending the insecurities that plagued my heart and soul. For ten years, we danced in the realm of pure happiness, our love radiating with undeniable brilliance. He taught me to trust, to believe in the transformative power of affection, and to embrace the magnificent journey of self-discovery.

But alas, as time unfurled its bittersweet wings, we realized that the beauty of our love had served its purpose. It had nurtured and healed, and now it was time to release each other, to honor the callings of our individual souls.

The memories we shared remain as sparkling gems, etched upon the needlepoint of my existence. They remind me of his profound impact on my life, the lessons learned, and the growth attained. He healed me, not only from men's insecurities, but also from the depths of my vulnerabilities.

And so, we part ways, forever transformed by the love we shared. With hearts overflowing with gratitude, we stepped into the unknown, embracing the vastness of life, ready to discover new chapters, new adventures, and new opportunities for love to touch our lives once again.

During this trying time, my mother, Athena, became my inner strength, motivation, and the reason behind my recovery from that man. Little did she know, as I have never really told her.

You see - I did not have a father role model. In that manner, I did not know the difference between a man and a boy. It took me years to figure this out.

While travelling, reading, writing, moving to different places, and working for diverse jobs and countries, I began finding myself.

I knew a day would come when I would find my true inner self and purpose, and all I wanted would come to reality; I didn't know when and how. During trying times, Maya Angelou's poem *Alone* ignited me with a sense of strength to find myself back. Please do yourself a favour and look up the poem and read it. I wish I could have placed it here, but it would violate the copyright of the poet.

For many years, no matter what I did or how I felt, an ever-expanding void, a profound sense of emptiness, took root, often consuming me and steadily enveloping my very being. No matter what I pursued or experienced, the emptiness persisted, gnawing at my soul, and expanding its influence with relentless determination. Its grip on me grew stronger daily, leaving me increasingly trapped within its depths as if I were being swallowed whole by an abyss.

I constantly kept myself occupied, trying to distract myself from the void and seeking fulfillment in every way. Yet, despite my efforts, the emptiness persisted, expanding relentlessly daily. It endured for an extended period, stretching several years, until a remarkable shift occurred within me. During this time, I discovered the unexpected pleasure that could be derived from simply doing nothing—finding solace and a sense of contentment in moments of stillness and quiet reflection.

> "Beyond the edge of the world, there's a space where emptiness and substance neatly overlap, where past and future form a continuous, endless loop. And, hovering about, there are signs no one has ever read, chords no one has ever heard."**— Haruki Murakami, Kafka on the Shore**

Despite the endless loop, for the outside world watching my existence, I was doing better than great, often described as a pure and rather raw genius. The dating scene was spectacular! Lots of attention, but nothing seemed to grasp my interest at heart, keeping me going for long. I travelled the World, had various jobs, met a lot of people, created amazing friendships, and thought that by initiating new beginnings; I would find my inner peace, voice, and, ultimately, some happiness…The more I moved upward in the world, the less I could relate to it. I saw nothing at all – just a hollow devouring me.

This marked when I embarked on a journey of volunteering, dedicating my time to assist the homeless, abused, neglected children, and battered women. Through this selfless act of service, I discovered a newfound sense of purpose, a way to make a positive impact on the world.

As I spent hours immersed in the lives of those grappling with severe challenges, I witnessed a transformation within myself. The gaping void that had plagued me gradually dissipated, overshadowed by the stark realities faced by others. It became evident that the obstacles I once deemed significant paled compared to the pragmatic issues endured by these individuals.

At the time, I worked in finance at one of the most prominent financial and media institutions ever established in New York. From my observations, people would gladly take my place with an envious look. At barely 24, I had more than they worked their whole lives.

And contrary to misconceptions, luck or good fortune had not simply bestowed itself upon me. In truth, I wrought tirelessly to attain my position and all that I have achieved. I invested immense effort and dedicated countless hours to my pursuits, leaving no stone unturned in my relentless quest for success. The accomplishments I proudly claim were not mere strokes of luck or reference but the hard-earned rewards of my unwavering determination and relentless labor.

As I grew, I went furiously into consulting and transferred through jobs. I saw the world evolve, but no matter the pursuit, it seemed my daily work was only meant to pay the bills.

During my volunteering time, I woke up one of my dead brain cells, finally murmuring to myself, "How could one possibly represent one conglomerate after the next without specifically serving any social corporate responsibility angle?"

The more I dedicated my time to representing these giants, the more I would lose my grounding. Things would go from complete blur to crystal clear. My awakening became a curse and ideological motivation. Initially, I thought I had completely lost it. I was only awakening.

I was unsure and a bit on air, skeptical about what was right or wrong, where I should work, and how to better deal with my relationships.

To make the story short, I found no interest whatsoever. I felt everything was fleeting – lacking substance and quickly had to move from one chapter to the next until I could fill that void.

All was well-an excellent job, living the good life, sharing it with a man I really cared about. While it was all exciting, or at least it felt that way, here comes the cheating part-stunned and heartbroken, I couldn't get it out of my system. I could not believe it - what a slap!

Such hits under the belt take the air you breathe, leaving you shuttered and never recovering. Time passes, and some pieces come together, but you are never whole again.

Ultimately, I lost faith - assuming and wrongly conditioning myself to believe this would happen with all my relationships. And guess what? It did. It became a consistent nightmare, yet another crash and then another.

With every impact, my conscious level raised to a different frequency. Simultaneously, I realized that my choices of men did not match my worth. I had subliminally convinced myself it was better to feel safer with someone you could control.

Surprisingly, these men carried their baggage and used me to fill their void or validate their pitiful existence. Sometimes, they tried to make me feel bad so they could feel better, which is where I would usually snap and leave them in the cold.

Initially, I could not understand the whole rollercoaster and adversity, but in retrospect, I wanted to learn more about them. When they felt relieved and at ease and a little more comfortable in my presence or possibly thinking that they had me at their fingertip, they would try to tear me down to feel superior. This is the point where they would see my other self – much darker, distant, and self-sufficient, bringing them to their knees, no matter how I felt inside.

The relentless repetition of the same vicious cycle persisted across all my relationships, each becoming more agonizing than the last. But then again, it was not for long. There came a pivotal moment when I could abruptly sever its grip swiftly.

After engaging in two discussions on the precipice of the third, I summoned the courage to liberate myself from the suffocating confines of the relationship once and for all. In a decisive instant, I severed the ties that had bound me, embracing a future free from the toxic patterns that had haunted me for far too long. For a communicator, I was not successfully communicating, at all – just acting, moving, and shuttering others and me on the way.

The pain cut deep, yet I forged ahead without glancing back. My intention was never to pass judgment or inflict harm upon these men. Still, it was driven by the fear I harbored within and what I believed to be the best course of action for my own well-being.

At that moment, I made a choice guided by self-preservation, recognizing the need to prioritize my needs and aspirations above all else. While it was a difficult decision, I held onto the belief that by embracing my path, I could nurture a future that had true confidence, happiness, and fulfillment.

Peter T. McIntyre quotes, "Confidence comes not from always being right but from not fearing to be wrong."

Looking back to my life partners, they truly healed me from my nemesis but were never meant to be there for the long run. I knew that part entirely from the start.

Similarly, to how my father had left us early on, I was inflicting the same harm to avoid the pain that I already knew was coming - one way or another.

In my quest to find myself, I realised that I wasn't truly embodying my authentic self within those relationships. I could only muster about twenty-five percent of my time and attention, leaving most of it ambiguous. As for the remaining moments, do not ask where I was or what I was doing, for it was a dark realm I preferred to keep undisclosed. During those undisclosed moments, I sought solace, introspection, and the space to explore my identity, unburdened by the expectations and dynamics of the relationships I was entangled in.

Nonetheless, I persisted in my journey of self-discovery. I ventured across various paths through travel, study, and work, each leading me closer to uncovering my inner truth. Yet, despite my endeavors, when I stood before the mirror and gazed upon my reflection, the answers remained elusive, as if written on a blank canvas. The precise moment when I resolved to embrace solitude and find myself eluded me, but I recognized that a single day had the power to ignite profound change. Within the stillness of my dark company, I embarked on a transformative path, seeking to unravel the mysteries that lay dormant within me.

There were men I dated from time to time, but nothing too serious. Anything too serious would suffocate me.

Meanwhile, the more I dated, the greater the void. Funny enough, I had different types and ages of men pursuing me. When I needed to be alone, I attracted more men to my cycle.

Moving from one country to the next, from the USA, Brussels, Luxembourg, Switzerland, and Athens, I finally found myself in London.

Everything seemed difficult and quite dark there. The job scene was severe, and the boy-scene was entirely boring. The outing was borderline suicidal, while the job scene relentlessly nauseating!

People were weird, and everything was unlikeable-at least to my taste and character.

The good news was that I found myself in a beautiful house with a great flat-mate and making amazing friends. Irrevocably, I found myself at ease, where I could be myself, focus, and figure out the next steps in my life.

That present moment took a toll on memory lane, reflecting on my past experiences and accomplishments, my happiness, flaws, shame, disappointments, breakups, makeups, lonely days, heartbreaks, judgments, lonesomeness, and unsatisfactory results to finally press the f… restart button.

Before I could grasp it, I went from one self-development class to the next. Joining "AA" seminars when I wasn't even an Alcoholic made me realise, to an extent, the changes needed.

That part was hilarious and not quite funny, especially when you had to own up to saying something you are not. I am an "AA" and have been sober for the past ten days.

When I considered it, sobriety could also mean a dozen other things. And if I were living a two-sided life story, how could I convince myself of being sober? I would get up and say, "Hey, group, this is enlightening; I am not only an AA, but I also don't know who I am. Please help me."

One after the next, they did. And there it was, my awakening journey started picking up. "It must never be forgotten that the purpose of Alcoholics Anonymous is to sober up alcoholics. There are no religious or spiritual requirements for membership. No demands are made on anyone. An experience is offered, which members may accept or reject. That is up to them," Bill W. says.

Chapter 2

Embrace Your Extraordinary and Move Beyond Pain and Fear

Are you facing fears? One kind of statement and then comes another one. Stop stacking up your feelings under the carpet and face the accumulated pain today. As Napoleon Hill used to say, "Fears are nothing more than a state of mind."

What are you afraid of? The reality was losing myself in reacting when simultaneously feeling fear and pain! In such feelings, I knew that fear and pain were the same coin. "Whatever you fear causes you great pain." The more you are in pain, the more remarkable that fear becomes. During that process and acknowledging all the little things that hurt me, I gradually found myself. I would smile but intensively cry inside—a regrettable pain in a lesson.

I appeared okay, but I was screaming inside. I would say everything is fine, but nothing got any better. This became the exact point of masking and concealing everything, one situation after another. Then, one day, we wake up and scream and say, "Who am I? Where am I going? I am not happy."

The most significant part of our pain is self-inflicted. We allow problems to suck the life out of us, and given that our conscious levels are low, that pain affects us immensely. Although our energy vibration may be down at the time, and fear has found us vulnerable, we feed on our vital energy to further debilitate us. Being in pain becomes familiar; we begin to identify and become comfortable around it, and it adds more to it. However, clearly understanding what fear does to us, it has been my choice to remain or regain my strength and stand my ground.

In the words of the great Nelson Mandela, "I understand that courage is not the absence of fear, but the triumphant conquest over it. The true embodiment of bravery is not someone who never feels afraid, but one who rises above their fears and emerges victorious."

And oh, the invaluable lesson that has been bestowed upon me in this realm of courage and resilience comes from none other than my current partner.

Ah, this extraordinary being who has the uncanny ability to ignite both my anger and my heart with a fiery passion. During it all, he shines with a radiance that astounds me.

No matter his challenges, he chooses to adorn the world with smiles, jokes, and a contagious aura that leaves everyone a little happier in his wake. It's as if nothing can dim his light, even though he could easily offer many excuses. His inner beauty mirrors his outward appearance, for he possesses a rare depth that captivates my soul.

I am mesmerized by his unwavering spirit, infectious laughter, and ability to maintain a genuine smile wherever he goes. This man, a father of two, has weathered the storms of life with both serious and severe ups. Yet, his eyes retain turquoise blue, green, and yellow purity and clarity. His smile, an emblem of his conquest over the world, radiates a warmth that envelops all in its embrace.

What astonishes me is that he remains blissfully unaware of the immense power he holds within. Such potential, fearless and untamed, resides within him. Yet, he humbly carries himself with an earthy charm that touches my heart. He possesses vulnerabilities, scattered here and there, that add to his relatability and make him more endearing in my eyes.

Oh, the wonder of witnessing this amazing soul navigate through life, conquering the world with a strength he may not even realize he possesses. He embodies the essence of fearlessness, encapsulating the spirit of triumph over adversity. And in his presence, I am filled with boundless admiration, love, and respect for the magnificent human being he is.

So, here's to my partner, a beacon of light in my life, a reminder that courage lies not in the absence of fear but in the unwavering determination to rise above it. Together, we embark on a journey where love intertwines with courage, vulnerability dances with strength, and the triumph of the human spirit knows no bounds; plus, we both hate cheating, which is huge!

I am discussing this part as any boy or man was relatively fleeting before my current relationship. It ended up leaving abruptly or getting cheated on before finding the courage to enter the relationship. Being cheated on meant that I was not good enough. Leaving the relationship meant that I could not be me and ended up suffocating until I would explode. In all honesty, though, these men were only there to heal and raise my consciousness and not necessarily make me happy for the longer term.

During those short-term partnerships or a few dates, we simply taught each other some lessons that would raise our consciousness to move on with our lives.

Obviously, for some time and while in the relationship, I had idealized my partners based on my need to be in a relationship. Eventually, after I had raised them to those standards, my downfall became greater. They say all girls do this one way or another 'we will fix them.' "We love them enough to fix them," they murmur and drink.

In the bigger picture - these great men were never really part of my long-term life plan. They were to add and take from my life, which became my stronghold in the long run. To learn something else - to find something entirely different. Evidently, at that point, I was resisting the virtual certainty that these people were not for me in the first place. Again, all young, old, and older girls do the same thing and repeat the same cycle.

My mother, Athena, had always put it right, "Never look at the ground to find what you should be looking up. When you are up, they are always down. When you bring them up, they want you down, and you were never meant to look down!" Damn, how right she was!

In all truth, my two cents of wisdom belong to my mother by at least half! But it is also true that we never acknowledge our mothers initially. Growing up I thought she was judgmental and never backed me. But she backed me up with all her means until her last breath.

In time and experience, she still says you would need to apply standards in your life. "If you want something better in your life, you will need to find yourself the love that you want for you. It is not really going to knock on your door."

Then again, love is blind. Sometimes, you will love somebody's eyes, how they articulate themselves, possibly their dynamic, charming, witty character, sensual appeal, power or money and other such characteristics that may not even match your standards.

At the end of the day, it is all about your total package and theirs and how the two strike a balance, which does not mean downplaying yourself and your needs to fit other people's precepts.

To do this, you would need to understand the residue of your past's pain and how far you would go settling or compromising to reach your happiness. My motto in life has been, "No settling!"

Deep inside, my innermost belief was that everyone would leave as my father did, which had manifested as a continuous pattern without even recognising it. Given that fear, I was never present in my relationships because I feared losing more if I did.

During my healing, I gave way for someone else to be in my life who was willing to give more. Not having such a relationship before, I started to doubt whether meeting someone genuine would ever become a reality.

Ah, the intriguing notion of abstaining from relationships altogether, believing that we could shield ourselves from the sting of heartache by severing emotional connections. It sounds rather tempting, doesn't it? But oh, the madness of such a mental state breeds a gathering storm of pain and bitterness that festers within our very being.

At first, it may lie dormant, lurking beneath the surface like a dormant volcano, but oh, the slightest remark or trigger can awaken its fiery wrath. Suddenly, we find ourselves on the defensive, bracing for impact with everything that comes our way. Pain seems to permeate every corner of our existence, convincing us that no matter our path, it will inevitably lead to anguish. It's as if the pain has become an unwanted companion, forever whispering in our ears.

Yet, amidst this tempest of emotions, we must remember that pain and fear only possess as much power as we willingly bestow upon them. They are like unruly guests who thrive on our attention and identification. Our unconscious association with these emotions allows them to survive and thrive.

But, my dear friend, we are not powerless in this dance. We can shift our perspective, reclaim our agency, and redefine the course of our experience. Pain and fear may knock on our door, but we can choose whether to invite them or send them packing.

For any problem to flourish, it must find a willing host within our hearts and minds. So, let us shift our focus and embrace the power of positivity, determination, and a fiery spirit that refuses to be consumed by negativity. Let us consciously identify with the feelings that bring us joy, hope, and resilience.

In this dance of life, we must acknowledge that pain and fear are not the natural course of action. They are temporary visitors who may leave their mark but need not define our entire journey. We can create a different experience filled with laughter, love, and the unwavering determination to rise above adversity.

So, my friend, release the grip of accumulated pain and bitterness. Open the door to the light, to the humor that brings a sparkle to your eyes and a skip to your step. Embrace the power within you, and let it guide you towards a path where the pain is but a fleeting visitor, unable to overshadow the brilliance of your spirit.

Identifying with pain means that you must let that feeling turn into thinking, the thinking into judgment, and the judgment into resistance, leading to pain and fear taking over you, eventually becoming you. Have you heard that thoughts become things one way or another?

Convictions such as anger, hatred, grief, drama, violence, and even illness are closely linked to your fears and pain, which is nothing but a state of mind.

The energy and intensity rise in correlation to your worries and problems. Therefore, it is essential to acknowledge that state of disharmony and denial that you find yourself in. Observe the resistance and the attachment to your pain to enhance your alertness.

Perceive if you enjoy being unhappy and notice if you overtly discuss it. Now see through it and accept it for what it is. Witness it and start breaking it down for what it is, resulting in your light of consciousness and helping you face your fears and all your pains.

Otherwise, if you don't, you will relive it in one way or another as life manifests in circles and repetitions until you get the lesson you are supposed to learn and move on. It has happened to me, and I am still trying to understand how I can be that foolish when all I need to do is simply face the truth and move in a different direction?

You simply need to raise that conscious level enough to understand things for what they are and gain back the resistance over your own presence.

Gaining your control means you have finally regained your inner strength, and your fears and pains can no longer be used against You!

Chapter 3

Ascending Above Your Mind

Growing up, despite my laser-focused attitude, I could not face any issues. When everything seemed to go with the flow, I was super happy. When things turn out sour, I would suffocate; breathe heavily, not sleep right or oversleep; not eating or over-indulging.

I could not think straight in the right senses and would feel the pain deeply before waking. When something went off, I would continuously have this mind-chatter reminding me of everything I did wrong—replaying the situation to understand what I could have done better.

I would cry my eyes out and get sick from my self-inflicted anxiety and stress levels. My mind-chatter and mental movies would go entirely overboard to the point of acting erratically. This state was nonexistent to none, not even my family, let alone my relationships.

During that time, I would close off from the world; put my perfect mask on; pretend that everything was okay, but everything was a pure mess. "There is always a part of the story missing when "they" write or talk about you. The face behind the mask is just not it all; we must see and feel everything. Wrongs don't define character; they build attitude and resilience," Ruby Karyo.

I did not face or discuss all that troubled me and created a long history of unresolved issues, whereby any problem that came along, despite its simplicity, added up to the previous point and got distorted. Instead of being my greatest cheerleader, I became my worst tormentor, with the capacity to attack, punish, and drain myself at every chance I got.

My mind was both my creator and destructor, leading me to happiness and bliss but also misery and disease. That latter became my wake-up call.

In 2011, my life took an unexpected turn, plunging me into a whirlwind of challenges and tribulations. It was during this tumultuous period that fate dealt me a cruel blow. This internal intestinal hemorrhage shook me to the core. The ensuing months brought about drastic changes in my life—my diet underwent a complete transformation, my working conditions became unbearable, and even my relationships suffered. It was a dark and uncertain time, filled with profound sadness, anxiety, and an overwhelming sense of impending doom.

I vividly remember the fear gripping my soul as I confronted the harsh reality that this could end my journey. The doctors' grim prognosis lingered in my mind like a haunting specter, constantly reminding me of the fragile thread on which my life hung. It was a terrifying wake-up call, a stark reminder that if I continued down the same treacherous path, my existence would be extinguished within a mere two years.

Amidst the despair, a glimmer of hope emerged, bringing a second chance at life. This newfound opportunity propelled me to take drastic measures and confront my deepest fears head-on. The threat of mortality became an unexpected ally, forcing me to examine my thoughts and unravel the intricate web of self-deception that had ensnared me for far too long.

I learned that when you listen to the whispers of your own mind, you simultaneously become aware of its power and influence over your being. As each thought echoed through the corridors of my consciousness, I bore witness to its existence and acknowledged its presence. In this conscious awareness, the thoughts began to lose their grip, gradually fading into insignificance until they vanished altogether. I had finally evicted those insidious notions that had plagued me for years, freeing myself from their suffocating hold.

In this liberation, a profound transformation occurred.

I stepped into the radiant embrace of my true self, basking in the glow of enlightenment and inner peace. The weight of anxiety and drama that had burdened me for so long lifted and was replaced by a newfound sense of purpose and tranquility. The scars of my past experiences constantly reminded me of the strength I possessed and the resilience that defined me.

Now, as I reflect upon that tumultuous chapter of my life, I am reminded of the profound journey I embarked upon—a journey marked by humor, and spice, but also sadness, anxiety, and gripping drama. It was through the crucible of adversity that I discovered the depths of my spirit and embraced the gift of a second chance—a chance to live, to thrive, and to savor each precious moment. A second chance to breathe in peace.

With practice, this peace will deepen, and so will your joy and sense of harmony arise. During that state, as you continue to use your brain as a tool that is on your side, you become a defender to gather, store and analyze information instead of letting it attack you to hinder your growth and potential, causing a severe leakage to your vital energy.

Chapter 4

Getting Rid of your own Negativity and Drama

"Only you and you alone can change your situation. Don't blame it on anything or anyone," Leonardo DiCaprio said. Who said Leonardo is not but a pure genius? Now, gaining that inner peace does not mean you are getting rid of your mind-chatter but emitting negativity and drama resulting from fears, problems, and pains.

This negativity and drama are usually a result of assumptions and perceptions over certain situations that we have failed to resolve, or they could be "self-created" situations. In any case, we unconsciously bring these elements into our thoughts and imaginations. Such factors control our lives to a degree that carries a heavy burden of the past into our current lives and refuse to let go.

From my perspective, it is more like putting on a jail ankle bracelet from day one, which can eventually control your life. Your mind is the worst jail that you can ever be! Believe it or not, that state of mind will carry on to your future, no matter the change in surroundings or any material belongings you acquire. One of the greatest women ever lived, Oprah Winfrey, boldly said, "The struggle of my life created empathy-I could relate to pain, being abandoned, having people not loving me."

In other words, no matter how intense the pain afflicts, the combination of negativity will translate to an enormous drama that will contribute to your character and attitude. Eventually, you become overwhelmed by life situations and lose your sense of being. We create more problems and drama when we have enough time. To clarify, we overestimate these everyday life problems as threatening emergencies, which inevitably lead to the emergency room.

On the contrary, when we go through a life-threatening situation, the mind automatically sojourns to focus on the present as your life is at stake and can only be better when we eliminate this crucial state by not adding more to what's already happening. As mentioned before, when there is a situation or an issue, what's the point in elevating it and making it worse? If it makes you anxious, what is the need to add sadness, bitterness, and unforgiveness to feel worsened? We both know that doesn't improve the condition but makes it much worse!

Logically, when the situation gets worse in your mind, the only person doing it is you! You control your thoughts, and you can change them. If that's not the case, then you are only drawing more drama to your life and continuously repeating the same patterns.

Unbeknownst to me, I reached a stage where my self-perception became increasingly distorted, gradually eroding the core of my identity. Unwittingly, I found myself detached from the essence of who I was, failing to recognize the destructive pattern that had silently corroded my life over an extended period. It was a revelation that struck me with profound impact, as I realized how much this pattern had subtly undermined my sense of self and led me astray from living an authentic and fulfilling existence.

Does it feel scary when there is less drama in your life, or do you love the stress out of it? And if so, how can you change the situation when you keep repeating past failures?

When you accept the attraction of negativity and drama stem, which is an attachment to the past, pessimism will continue to grow, and the problems will be left unsolved. Therefore, resulting in an eternal state of misery, creating more problems and unwanted circumstances with no solutions, will irrevocably deny your present. Am I right here?

When you deny your present, you fail to recognise your surroundings and not realising what's going on around your circle.

When you fail to use your senses, you are not observant, not touching, acknowledging, and not breathing. You are truly lost and just passing by. When you refuse to see the answers and keep asking the questions, the possibility of appreciating life for what it is becomes blank.

Life isn't all doom and gloom, my friend. In fact, it's like a buffet of flavours, waiting for you to dig in and savour every delicious moment. So, let's sprinkle some humour and spice into your existence and uncover the true meaning of living in the now!

Picture this. You're standing at the doorway of your own vivacity, ready to unleash your inner party animal. But, uh-oh, a sneaky little troublemaker is lurking in the shadows—the negativity and drama that your mind conjures up like a magician with a twisted sense of humour. It's time to pull the curtain on that illusion. Imagine your distorted mind as a wacky time-lapse video, distorting reality like a funhouse mirror. It's like watching a comedy skit gone wrong, with your negativity and drama stealing the spotlight and leaving you feeling like the punchline. But fear not, for the power to live your best life is in your hands—or in your mind.

You need to do a mental double-take, a grand snap out of that destructive state of mind hijacking your happiness. It's as simple as making a choice—embracing the positive energy bubbling inside you, just waiting to be unleashed like a confetti cannon at a celebration.

So, let's break it down: Life's not about being a perpetual party pooper. It's about grabbing opportunities like a kid grabbing candy at Halloween with a mischievous grin plastered on your face. Shake off the negativity, dust off those drama-shoes, and step into a world where laughter is the currency and humour is your secret weapon. When you seek deeper into the nooks and crannies of your existence, you'll discover that life is an adventure filled with hidden treasures of joy, love, and laughter.

So, let's rewrite the script and turn your life into a blockbuster comedy that leaves you rolling on the floor with laughter, spicing up every moment with a pinch of humour and a dash of audacity.

Remember, the choice is yours. Will you let the comedy of life tickle your funny bone, or will you continue to let negativity steal the show? It's time to grab the mic and be the comedian of your own story. Get ready to embrace the spice, the humour, and the sheer absurdity of it all – my current partner has taught me that wild and clear! Your life is waiting, so let's go out there and rock the stage!

Otherwise, Life will keep repeating itself in continuous f. loops, no matter the circumstances, situations, or issues. So, regardless of any situation, you need to tell yourself that it is your conscious choice to no longer create pain for yourself, not repeat the same loop and simply let go and accept all life, f. situations, issues, and challenges as they come - trying to find solutions that will change your current state for the better, but not necessarily crying over that spilt milk, damn it! Why give that power to something that, in reality, is relatively small? How will you react to something that comes and is seriously bad?

My life mantra is that you owe it to yourself to push you beyond any limitations; you have that power of choice— to feel completely fed up with your suffering. Just shock your way out of it, and you will soon see that no specific barriers or obstacles will have the power to act as negative catalysts that can actually ground you from living fully. "And now that you don't have to be perfect, you can be good," said John Steinbeck.

Chapter 5

Stop Your Ego from Ruling Your Life

While growing up, our daily struggles found ourselves close to the Sun; a sanctuary to find our closure. It could be living or moving to a different country, meeting your soulmate, getting accomplished in a job, or carrying on a rewarding career. Having kids, living a happy, fulfilled life in harmony.

As part of our progress, we begin to educate ourselves, going to school, college, then Universities, and moving on with our professional paths. We all have aspirations, expectations, and goals - our internal and external thoughts come from our family structures. All these elements support the positive side of our egos, which is integral to our growth and potential. However, at some point in our lives, our egos get confused with pride. We begin identifying ourselves with titles, money, cars, houses, statues, and so forth, forgetting our real and natural identity.

In other words, we feel that success is to receive an "X" amount of money every month, and unless we get to that point, we are not happy. "Money is numbers, and numbers never end. If it takes money to be happy, your search for happiness will never end," Bob Marley said.

When it comes to a relationship, when we do not have that type of love in our lives, then we never really feel respected or appreciated. Most unfortunate people may think that unless they drive a specific type of car or go to Bora Bora for their vacation, they will not succeed.

Driven by society's standards, we verge on having a distorted sense of reality in our minds. To achieve our inner wants, we must boost our ego and feelings, closely associated with how the world perceives us.

When we strive for all these fundamentals, we get to the point of wanting more and more of the same material things to retain our happiness and end up never feeling happy as we become slaves of these unfulfilling needs.

Similarly, to our relationships with other people, from a friendship or a partnership angle, we seek people that satisfy such criteria. Despite our family standards, as we move on in life, we get to live by other measures, usually by association with friends, lovers, and sometimes feeling brainwashed by societal standards. In the end, we can't run from people. Albert Einstein once said, "Try not to become a man of success. Rather become a man of value."

When we put all that into perspective, who are we? What is right or wrong? Every movement of our lives is a brainwashing mechanism to act in a certain way, the so-called norms. Oprah Winfrey is right once again, saying, "When you undervalue what you do, the world will undervalue who you are."

Depending on the relationships we have established, our ego further standardises the realm and direction of our life. And as we move along, these ego standards play the primary role, given that the brain manipulates the ego, and the mind game begins!

Everything becomes a win-or-lose situation. The more you win, the happier you are. The more you lose, the sadder you become. When you have more wins than losses, you cuddle in bed and sleep well at night. The more losses you have, the worse your sleep becomes. Sounds familiar? And for some years, this may be your reality. It could seem okay for the most part, but nothing fulfills you.

As time progresses, you get lonelier by the day. You feel a void of emptiness, an empty heart, and a strong sense of neglect that no one possibly thinks or cares for you. You don't seem to enjoy anything unless you have a drink or two most of the time.

Sometimes, you may go to the edge of finding happiness and harmony and even decide to have different partners for excitement, but nothing works.

You choose to drink every night, hear lousy music, or go to lunch or dinner with friends or people you have just encountered to avoid or fill that void.

When the fun finally pulsates, you find yourself back at the house and feeling drained with a wholesome emptiness; the void never left but was temporarily stroked.

From the New Republic report dated May 13th, 2013, loneliness from a psychological definition hasn't changed since Fromm-Reichman proclaimed the adversities. "Real loneliness," as she called it, is not what the philosopher Soren Kierkegaard characterized as the "shut-upness" and solitariness of the civilized. Nor is "real loneliness" the happy solitude of the productive artist or the passing irritation of being cooped up with the flu while all your friends go off on some adventure.

It's not being dissatisfied with your companion of the moment- your friend or lover or even spouse- unless you chronically find yourself in that situation, in which case you may be lonely. Loneliness, she said-and will surprise no one - the want of intimacy.

Returning to our discussion, I've been blessed to understand certain things quite early, whereas most of my age mates didn't. Still, I also had fears of insecurities, negativity, and pains associated with my egoic mind, letting these elements control me for many years. When your ego takes you to a hostile place, lousy treatment of yourself or others, low self-esteem, and inner or outer abuse, it means that there is a deep-seated sense of lack or incompleteness of not being whole.

This state of mind is either conscious or unconscious. It was premeditated and had nothing to do with those circumstances, the wrong partners, and career orientation. Ah, the classic "sweep it under the carpet" technique. We've all been there. It's like trying to hide a herd of elephants in your living room, hoping no one notices. But let me tell you, that strategy has all the drama of a soap opera and none of the laughs.

Picture this: There's a problem knocking at your door, and instead of answering it head-on like a brave warrior, you choose to tango with your emotions. They waltz in and take over the dance floor, twirling you around in circles of confusion. It's like a melodramatic telenovela, with intense close-ups and dramatic background music. Confrontations? Oh no, no, no. They're as scary as that mysterious noise you hear in the middle of the night. You'd rather tiptoe around them, hoping they'll magically disappear like socks in the laundry.

But let me share a little secret with you: Confrontations aren't always as terrifying as they seem. In fact, they can be like deflating a balloon with a pin—lots of build-up, but the release is surprisingly relieving. Another great point my partner shares is, "Challenge me, and I will challenge you. I will love you more in the end!"

Deep inside, I hate confrontations as, in my distorted way, I fear being left alone again. So, let's talk about that fear of being left alone. It's like clinging to your partner like a koala to a eucalyptus tree, afraid that they'll vanish into thin air if you let go for a second. But trust me on this one - being alone is not the end of the world. In fact, it can be liberating, like finally getting to hog the entire tub of ice cream without any judgment. Embrace your own company, and you might discover that you're pretty good company after all.

And now, let's address the fear of never being good enough. It's like running in a hamster wheel, chasing an elusive sense of validation that's always out of reach. But guess what? You're more than good enough. You're a unique blend of awesomeness, splendidness, and quirkiness that nobody else can replicate. So, wave goodbye to that fear and strut your stuff like a peacock on a fashion runway.

In this grand comedy of life, it's time to drop the broom and face those problems head-on. Let the drama unfold, add a pinch of humor, and watch as you conquer each challenge like a true champion. You've got this! And remember, when life throws you a curveball, catch it, take a bow, and deliver a killer punchline. It's showtime!

So, to speak as bluntly as possible, when you are not transparent with your Being, you tend to seek everything else and then some more to fill in the void that remains within. Get it? Let me break it down. So, we all love that perfect slice of pizza, right? Despite always finding that ideal slide, I always tried to find a better one! WTF!

How is this possible? Someway, somehow the ingredients were all mixed up, still leaving me with a feeling that I may need another slice to make it all better. And before I knew it, I would be down with my fourth slice, then ice cream, then Coca-Cola Zero, and then a pill for the stomach to make it all go away.

The reality is different and much more straightforward - release all your wants and desires. You heard me right; let go, and don't get me wrong. I am not saying to stop working on yourself and your goals, but stop treating yourself as the mouse on the running wheel, never really getting the f. cheese! So, you need to change the mindset-how you see things.

When your egoic mind runs your life, you will never feel at ease, at peace, or fulfilled. The ego is a direct manifestation of external elements, so it will always crave more. And it must be continuously fed. But none of these external elements or possessions is you. So, the best way is to use them as tools, not vice versa.

At the same time, using these possessions equally means contributing more to your social setting and people in more vulnerable situations. Indeed, the more you make it in life, the only sense of fulfilment you will ever need is how you created a change in another person's life. This is why I founded my institute in the first place back in 2020 – and during a whole-blown pandemic! You heard me right!

Going to expensive restaurants, driving a nice car, using the latest technology, and wearing the most expensive clothes will mean nothing if you see a homeless child starving outside the restaurant and do nothing about it. Angelina Jolie knows that loud and clear. She has hugged and cared for more children than she can put in her house!

How about looking at a stray dog lying beside your Porsche, craving some warmth and doing nothing to help? Isn't Jane Fonda that helps relentlessly any animal that moves? Why do you think she does this? Buying the most expensive shoes for your little girl when a child just walked barefoot? How about recalling Lady Diana or

Audrey Hepburn and their impact on this world besides who they were?

Career recognition means nothing if your parents are not making enough money to make ends meet. Spending on your perfect plastic surgery is not your priority when the same money can be used to feed or help someone in need.

And as you may have guessed right, the only cause of making it further in life and faster made sense under the lenses of these contributions. All other options were not good enough, and precisely that part of me that will always be in check consciously. When I see myself getting a little less grounded, a little less humble, and less of a human, knowing I have enough time on my hands and misusing it, I turn to the other side to release some steam and creativity for the greater good. These checks and balances are a reality instilled in us from our mother.

I still recall when she bought food for other families and sent our clothes to nearby churches. To my detriment, even though finances were challenging at the time, we were still giving. My grandparents did the same, and my great-grandparents before that.

Going back in time, this was the best thing they could ever teach us-caring for other people and being compassionate, kind, generous, and authentic.

These elements always brought me back to square one-thinking of people less fortunate than me made me feel that no matter what, my most important possession is to be grateful for what I have and help others.

Being Human is the best association the egoic mind should have and strive for. From this point forward, everything else lacks both substance and importance, and it is all about temporary gratification. Coming to this realisation can partially heal your void by considering the following route: changing your life can only bear significance by creating more meaning for your life and others.

Chapter 6

Navigating the Love-Hate Rollercoaster: Lessons Learned

Reminiscing about my love-hate relationships, I admit, I've had a crystal-clear mindset about them – whether they were good or bad. No more going back and forth in situations that only bring heartache and misery. Life's too short for that nonsense!

Looking back, I realized I lacked some essential communication skills – being all dialectic and finding silver linings. It's like I was either in or out, with no in-between. A switch that goes either on or off, just like my past partner once said. My stubborn character has won me some battles, but it's also led to some epic losses.

But you know what? I've come to embrace it all as steppingstones, shaping the woman I am today. Life's funny like that – it throws some curveballs at you, and you either strike out or hit it out of the park!

And let me tell you, ladies, after going through hell and back, we're meant to take on the world! The universe tells us loud and clear, "Don't let others' judgments and opinions dictate your life. Be you, walk your path, and live it your way!" - Unknown. Preach, universe, preach!

Before diving headlong into any relationship, I've learned that I must first identify with my fabulous existence. We're attracted to similarities and intrigued by differences when we meet someone. And guess what? They influence each other, sometimes for better, sometimes for more drama.

But here's the kicker – without a strong foundation of self-love and acceptance, it's like mixing oil and water, resulting in a messy concoction of anger and bitterness. Let me tell you, ladies, we deserve better than that!

It's true; intimate relationships can be wild and passionate at first, like a rollercoaster ride of emotions and crazy lovemaking. But then, boom! Arguments, expectations, and overwhelming feelings swoop in, suffocating the romance. Homer nailed it when he said, "The heat of love, the pulsing rush of longing… irresistible – magic to make the sanest man, go mad." Oh, those insane rides!

You see, to have a real deal relationship, we've

got to be content with ourselves first. It's like finding that perfect pair of shoes – they must fit just right. Otherwise, you'll be walking around with blisters, and that's no way to strut your stuff!

Now, here's where it gets juicy. Most couples get addicted to the love-hate cycle, thinking it's normal drama. Let me tell you something – I'm not a fan of confrontations, so I make a break for it before things get too heated. Peace is my jam; anything disrupting that flow is not my cup of tea. Don't get me wrong, I've made my fair share of not-so-smart choices in the love department. Learned that the hard way. You can't claim to love someone and attack them simultaneously – love has no opposite! True love is like a gentle breeze on a summer day, not a thunderstorm wreaking havoc.

Speaking of love, let's talk destiny – I believe in love at first sight, and I've always felt a soul connection with that special someone meant for me. It's like our souls are doing a cosmic dance, destined to find each other even when the timing isn't right or life plays its tricks. But let me spill some honest tea – to experience that magical connection, you must let go of any emotional baggage weighing you down. So, I wrote a letter, poured my heart out to the universe, and then let it go. It's like decluttering your emotional closet – trust me, it's liberating!

I've learned some crucial lessons on this journey of love. Communication is the key – no bottling things up! The truth must be shared, even if it's a bit uncomfortable. And remember, love, should always be unconditional, like those two kids holding hands, skipping through life together.

So, here's my ultimate advice: don't make a relationship out of thin air. Just because someone knocks on your heart's door doesn't mean they're your forever person. Seek companionship, a partnership in crime, someone to share your wildest dreams and grow together. If it leads to marriage and kids, great! But if not, what matters most is connecting on the same wavelength. But hold on tight – for love to flourish, the light of your presence must outshine your ego and pains.

When both partners are conscious and accepting of each other, love transcends the mind and blooms like a rare flower in the heart. So, ladies, let's celebrate our journey of self-love and growth, and let love be the ultimate adventure! Trust me, we've got this, and the universe is cheering us on. Let's take on the world, one heartful stride at a time!

Chapter 7

Unleashing Your Inner Awesome Is a Rollercoaster Journey!

> "Life is not about achieving success; life is about unfolding yourself." **– Debasish Mridha**

Life is not just about checking boxes of success – it's about peeling back the layers of your awesomeness! As Debasish Mridha says, "Life is about unfolding yourself," and, let me tell you, it's a wild ride!

Finding that soul-deep connection with someone? It's not as easy as love at first sight or swiping right on a dating app. Nah-uh! It's a crazy concoction of communication, shared interests, personality sparks, and, yes, some serious sexual chemistry!

Hold up! Before you dive headfirst into a relationship, let me drop some truth bombs. Your priority, responsibility, and commitment should be to yourself first. Knowing your inner being is the secret sauce to a kickass relationship. Trust me on this one!

Let me keep it real – I won't pretend to be a guru of clarity and harmony. Nope! Fifty percent of the time, I'm like a walking bomb ready to go off! But hey, I've always had this fire inside me, a sense of responsibility and independence that made me the boss of my life from a young age. I might not have been the smartest "cookie" on the block regarding math. Those equations gave me panic attacks. But you know what? My cognitive skills were on point, and I had an eye for detail like nobody's business.

I have always had this abstract way of thinking – I had to create my structure of pure mess to make sense of things. Call it my superpower! But all this time, I'd pretend I had it all together. Ego mainly was talking, and boy, was it noisy! But you know what? I kept pushing myself to become a better version of me – personally and professionally. Like Denzel Washington says, "It's not about what you have; it's about who you've lifted, who you've made better." And that's what I aimed for!

Here's the thing – I'd question myself, get all quiet about stuff that bothered me, and then kaboom! I'd explode like a volcano. Confrontations weren't my jam, and chaos was a big no-no. But guess what? Disagreements can happen, and love can still thrive!

I had to learn the hard way – demand less, communicate more! Oh, and never bottle things up like grandma's secret recipe. Trust me, it's a recipe for disaster!

Do you want to know the secret sauce of personal growth? Hiccups! Yep, those little challenges are like hiccups – annoying, but they make you rethink your life's choices. Some people get more intense hiccups, like full-blown hurricanes, until they finally learn their lesson. But guess what? Those hiccups are steppingstones to greatness! Life's coding gets a bit wonky at first, but you find your inner harmony as you grow.

When your values align, magic happens – your mind, body, soul, and heart vibe in perfect sync. It's like a symphony of awesome! And when you reach that conscious level, you'll find peace within yourself. That's when you attract the right partner, the desired job, and all the good stuff! But don't be fooled, darling – it won't happen overnight. You must suffer a bit, hit rock bottom, and then rise like a phoenix! Embrace new thoughts, ditch the old baggage, and make way for your inner badass!

And let me tell you, when you let go, the struggle melts away like butter on hot toast. You'll find yourself connected like Wi-Fi to your inner harmony, and it's like a fresh new start! Joy, happiness, and awesomeness will come flooding your way!

So, it is time to unfold yourself, embrace your journey, and ride the rollercoaster of life with a big smile! It's a wild ride, but guess what? You're steering this ship, and it's time to rock this world – you owe it to yourself.

Chapter 8

Living in the Now Means Unboxing Your Life's Epic BS

> "I want to die living. And I want to be remembered as one who lived with purpose, joy and feeling, I want to spend my time learning what goes into a whole and happy life, then building that life the best I can." – **Steve Goodier**

Picture this. Life hands you a special gift box, but it's not just some ordinary present you can tear open on day one. Nah-uh! This beauty requires a bit of a wild ride before you can finally unwrap it and see what's inside.

You've got to level up, embrace the bumps, and even endure a bit of pain before you can claim that box as yours. But when you do, you might find yourself dancing in joy or scratching your head in confusion. It all depends on your mindset!

You'll look back and wonder, "Why didn't I realize my weaknesses earlier? Why did I take so long to figure this out?" We've all been there, questioning our past choices and wishing for a crystal ball. But here's the kicker – life doesn't give you all the answers upfront. Nope, it's like a sneaky game, pushing you to grow, learn, and become the fabulous version of yourself.

And guess what? You're in the driver's seat! You control your consciousness, mindset, and how you react to life's curveballs. Sure, it's tempting to think that one solution fits all, but life's a master at mixing up the ingredients!

Here's the real deal. The past is just a memory trace. And future-thinking? Nah, that takes you away from the real answer. The only reality you've got is the Now. Embrace it, hold it tight, and you'll level up your vibes like never before!

Living in the now means you'll radiate the energy of light like a cosmic disco ball! No more covering up with BS – it's time to embrace your true essence, connect with your being, and dance with your soul.

You'll be in a Zen state, meditating on positivity and waving goodbye to problems and suffering. Your new harmonious self will make you see the world in Technicolor. Flowers, trees, and skies are all vibing with you, and you'll realize how beautiful life is.

When you stop being a victim and wear your crown with pride, girl, you'll rock this world! Take charge, own your decisions, and stop letting negativity pull you down. You have three choices: change the situation, accept it, or runoff. Your call, boss lady! But whatever you choose, do it with mindfulness, transparency, and truthfulness. And here's the sweetest part – once you've unleashed your conscious decision-making skills, you'll break free from that endless cycle of negativity. Stress and fear? No room for those pesky guests!

So, let's raise that conscious level, shake off the drama, and unbox life's epic gift. It's time to live with purpose, joy, and feeling! Like Steve Goodier said, "I want to die living." And you know what? We'll be remembered for living our best, most fabulous life!

Chapter 9

Unleashing the Invincible You: Becoming Unbreakable no Matter what Life Throws on You

> "In theory there is a possibility of perfect happiness: To believe in the indestructible element within one, and not to strive towards it."- **Franz Kafka**

So, in terms of significance, what are you willing to do about it? Will you surrender to it or become resilient? Do you believe in the latter's possibility, or does it scare you to entertain such thoughts?

There was a period in my life when I was genuinely terrified of what to say and not to say. I felt like an eternal waiter, passively waiting for better things to come, lacking self-awareness, and perhaps even dwelling too much on the past. Instead of embracing the present, we often find ourselves constantly contemplating tomorrow. Henry David Thoreau once said, "You must live in the present, launch yourself on every wave, find your eternity in each moment. Fools stand on their island of opportunities and look toward another land. There is no other land; there is no other life but this."

We shy away from confronting reality in favour of clinging to our circumstances, ultimately leading us to become vulnerable and susceptible to harm. What if we could change that mindset once and for all?

Because of the heartaches that come with failed relationships, I used to resist going out with friends or getting to know new people. I preferred staying at home, sipping wine, and burying myself in books rather than taking a risk with someone new.

I lived in constant fear, but that time spent alone unexpectedly affected me. It transformed me in ways I had never imagined. I discovered I didn't need to go through countless experiences to comprehend what I needed to accept to move forward. Nevertheless, some of those experiences were undeniably harsh and could have been avoided. But then again, how else are you supposed to learn?

These lessons raise your consciousness and push you to do what is necessary for the now, leaving excuses aside. So, the answer is indeed in the Now.

There is no point in waiting to start living the Life you have always wanted while procrastinating until the ideal circumstances arise. There are no perfect situations, relationships, or events.

Everything in the universe is a work in progress, and that's a fact. When you let your mindset predict that perfect moment, nothing you do or achieve will ever be good enough. Then one day, something changes your current situation, and you cannot do what you wanted to do before.

Therefore, if you have 2, 3, or 50 things to do, start doing them no matter what, without thinking of the outcome. Stop living, wishing, procrastinating, complaining, and making excuses that only stop your present and prevent your future.

There is no point in using your energy without knowing what tomorrow holds. This illusion is projected onto reality, which builds an expectation for something great to happen. Even when that assumption becomes a realisation, and a dream comes true, the little mature steps and actions taken in your present brought you there in the future.

Still, without realising, you just bypassed a considerable chunk of your now to live in your future, which has not yet come and isn't even predictable.

Isn't that somewhat bothersome? What are you waiting to start living? Do you think you will always look the same, have the same energy, and feel the same?

Things evolve, people, the universe, autumn, fall, winter, time, and distance. Changes happen within you, around you, everywhere, and time never lapses.

No matter the money, position, status quo, and material things we acquire, we can never change back time.

In reality, we may indeed accomplish some quantity. Still, the quality of life has not changed, and the immediate, most profound need is to improve our existence as the foundation.

Once your understanding of this message is vivid and eye-opening, you automatically open new doors for the universe to take care of your Life, and any debilitating situation immediately improves. When you strive for the proper purpose, you substitute your comfort in life with current goals and expectations and accept nothing but the best.

It does not mean that change automatically happens when you don't work on them. But no matter the work you put into something, there is no way you will be able to create a superstructure.

Even when you create the perfect setting, this does not necessarily coincide with being happy with yourself, having the right person by your side, or improving your health. It takes a whole Life to create something and a moment to destroy it.

Everything in life should be regarded and not taken for granted. It is essential to cherish every moment, beginning with the little, simple, stupid pleasures - waking up with a smile, drinking your coffee on the balcony or garden, passing a good word and a blessing.

It is okay to have a relaxing salt bath, even when it takes a bit longer to leave the house; eat a healthy breakfast; go for a run in the morning; speak on the phone with family, friends, and loved ones, and send love to the people you care for. There are many things to do when you realise there is no time to waste. Isn't it a pity to look back and wished you had made changes instead of just doing them?

That is more or less how I began to rationalise everything. It was difficult, but I am taking that leap of faith here.

The awakening experienced was brought forth by a series of catalysts that propelled me forward. It was a period of introspection triggered by significant losses and a personal illness. Reflecting further, I wonder why we often need to reach such extremes before we wake up and start changing our lives? It requires cultivating gratitude and appreciation to break free from overthinking, over analysing, and tormenting ourselves with desires for what we lack or have never had.

Why do we focus so much on such unproductive thinking processes? What benefits does this level of thinking truly bring? Changing our mindset means acknowledging, cherishing, honour, and fully accepting our achievements alongside the challenges we have successfully endured. Giving ourselves recognition and praise wouldn't hurt, either. Our past challenges and choices undeniably shape who we are-they encompass one hundred percent of our being. Change is inevitable, but we must learn how to navigate through it.

However, finding fulfilment in what we have today, and our present actions alone won't lead to true fulfilment. If we lack fulfilment, a void will persist in our thoughts, eventually resulting in an empty feeling and a yearning for inner gratification.

No matter how many material possessions we accumulate, they won't bring lasting happiness. On the other hand, to become unbreakable, we must cultivate a sense of fulfilment through inner harmony and a clear sense of direction. Feeling grounded and secure in our capabilities, knowing that we can handle whatever comes our way while committing one hundred percent in each moment, fuels our motivation and boosts our creativity.

While in the company of friends and family, let us fully embrace each moment and make it memorable. When we are with someone special, let us create remarkable and unforgettable experiences. At work, let us find joy in doing what we do best. When we return home tired and exhausted, let us have a nourishing dinner, take a relaxing bath, and surrender ourselves to a peaceful sleep.

Sleep like a child and dream like a baby; you will always wake up nourished, youthful, and full of ideas!

Life is too precious and full of promises to be missed. There are good people in this world who need our help and support. We are all gifted, unique, and filled with life. It's better to seize each with determination rather than think of the life you could have had but never dared to grab it! Becoming unbreakable is a state of mind where we understand the distinction between our external and internal harmony.

Our external harmony drives us toward reaching our destination, guiding the steps we take and the decisions we make. Our inner harmony defines how we approach things and how they impact us in the present moment. By prioritizing how we feel and nurturing our inner harmony, we enhance the quality of our lives and gain clarity on the changes needed to fulfill our journey.

Therefore, let us focus on the present moment—our behaviours, reactions, mood swings, emotions, and fears. Strive to balance our inner and outer realities, allowing our inner harmony to radiate. In that state, we have mastered the lessons learned while knowing how to move forward.

In that graceful moment, the likelihood of being affected by external circumstances diminishes significantly as the strength of our inner harmony surpasses any situation or circumstance that may arise. The alternative is being at the mercy of every situation, identifying ourselves solely with external events to control our character. In such a scenario, we find ourselves trapped in a vicious cycle where nothing can overpower us except our own selves. As a result, nothing and no one can bring us down. "As you think, so shall you become." Because we believe in ourselves, we don't feel the need to convince others. Because we are content with ourselves, we don't seek others' approval. Because we accept ourselves, the whole world accepts us," said Lao Tzu.

Chapter 10

Mission Unlocked Embracing Your True North

> "Outstanding people have one thing in common: an absolute sense of mission."- **Zig Ziglar**

When I finally figured out the pieces to my life puzzle, I knew that creating my unbreakable shelf would equally mean creating or bringing some harmony into my life. Realistically, I've lived on a rollercoaster for the longest time and am always on edge. In many cases, I am still on edge, but it does not take the best of me. To find my true self, I had to loosen up and give more credit to myself and less to others. "Each of us is like a moon that shows only a few facets to earth, but never its full sphere," Andre Aciman.

Whatever I am today is due to a learning curve of trusting myself more and not necessarily letting others doubt me, no matter who they are. Finding my inner voice could only be possible through the experiences that led me to my current understanding of Life, people, and choices. But what seems like a lifetime to figure out, it is a day. That day that you would simply connect the dots.

The puzzle of who you are. What if other women have gone through the same path, similar or familiar? What if they cannot get back on track and fear puts them down? What if their insecurities are taking away their actual potential? What if their misery is self-inflicted, and it is not even related to any surrounding, person, or people? What if they need the drama to get them going? What if their past mistakes are debilitating them to the point of not living their present?

Considering these questions led me to believe that I had a mission and had to do something about it. With grace and utmost humility, I started putting my thoughts down till I could conclude this book, "The Woman's Circle of Harmony." With such consideration and turn, I gave my two cents of thoughts and opinions, which circles back to not just me and my family of women but possibly most women I have known and met.

My story will hopefully plant the seeds of tomorrow's reactions from every single woman I know, and I will get to know in the future. For me, it is sufficient that one thought or statement will be used as an embarkment to something magnificent that will follow and considered in our own sense of timing.

Some women are brave and bold enough to give their objectives; for many, they may even start opening up or start again and again, till they get exactly what they deserve: harmony within, which they can then pass to their inner and outer circle of women.

Others may feel that their story is personal and should not be discussed openly because of the fear associated with judgment, shame, disappointment, and disgrace. They will still get to that harmony, but later in life, they simply had to go through their own unique lessons to arrive at different conclusions and set their life to another standing.

Others may choose to deny and defend their actions, judging and questioning, "Who am I to tell them how to be and what to do?" In fact, I am not asking you to speak to me, but to yourself. Communicate with yourself, your church, your counsellor, a friend, or a community group to help you through your healing journey and enable your path to move on to better things ahead of you. When you acknowledge that something is up, and unless your fear and denial keep you locked, you will quickly recognise the issues and the need to do something about it.

Whatever feels better for you, such as reading a book, going to the gym, meditating, jogging, etc. – use it to open your horizons to discuss all that matters openly to you. Reaching out privately or publicly is the first step honouring yourself and acknowledging a situation of hurt, denial, neglect, pain, abuse, death, and finding peace and strength.

I am here to take you from inaction to some action, an unhappy place to a happy one, as I have been there and gone through the same – not once, but many times. Does this make me an expert? No. It makes me a woman, just like you, with the same vulnerabilities, fears, scars, challenges, and heartaches that decided that I deserved more from life and simply stood up to get it.

Moving from a mediocre life to absolute fulfilment, a cynical mindset to a harmonious one. From a self-destructive mode to a creative one. From an introvert to an extrovert. From a staller to moving forward no matter what.

From a stagnant situation to growth. So, what is it going to be for you? The choice is in your hands, but be mindful that you deserve to find true friendship, love, joy, happiness, family, and a home. You too deserve to feel fulfilled. In my relentless quest for harmony and to share its wisdom with the world, I'm on a mission to bring balance to myself and to you and all the incredible women out there. It's a journey of contribution and commitment to the greater good, transcending the narrow confines of our own lives.

Oh, let me tell you, my path to understanding and embracing the true essence of womanhood was no walk in the park. I had to dive headfirst into a labyrinth of self-help and self-development processes, navigating the twists and turns to reach where I stand today – ready to uplift and unite women at a higher level of consciousness.

You know what? I genuinely believe that knowledge and evolution are meant to be shared, not hoarded like the last piece of chocolate in a household full of kids! Positivity, my dear, is like a contagious dance - we've got to spread it like wildfire! As for negativity, it deserves a one-way ticket to oblivion – release it and let it disintegrate into the ether!

But alas, I've witnessed too many women carry the weight of pain as if it's the latest fashion accessory. This heavy burden becomes woven into the fabric of their identity. It clings to them, manipulating their every step, like an uninvited guest that never leaves.

And here's the tragic part – they often keep their feelings locked away in a vault, collecting dust for days, months, and even years! It's like they're running a museum of unsaid emotions, and it takes a lifetime for them to finally release what has been brewing all along.

Then, when the dam of truth finally breaks, it's like an epic eruption of volcanic emotions. I mean, imagine a tea kettle's whistle transforming into a full-blown fireworks display – that's what it's like! I am sure we have all experienced it, right?

Now, picture this – I've surrounded myself with remarkable women, fiercely successful and relentlessly driven. They are conquering the world and providing for their families, but deep down, they're discontented, disconnected, and, dare I say it, unhappy.

It is as if they are carrying a colossal burden on their shoulders, slowly weighing them down. But here is the heartbreaking part – they often realize the damage they have done to themselves much later in life, like a realization that dawns in their 60s, 70s, or even closer to the time they mingle with the stars as earth dust.

But my dear friends, it doesn't have to be this way! We can release the weight, let go of the pain, and dance to a different rhythm – a rhythm of unbridled joy and fulfilment. So, let's stand tall, support each other, and create a symphony of empowerment and unity. It's time to be the fierce warriors we were born to be, breaking free from the chains that have held us back for far too long.

As we embark on this journey together, let's laugh louder, love deeper, and lift each other higher. For we are not just women - we are the architects of our destiny, the authors of our story, and the bearers of the most magnificent force in the universal melody – the indomitable spirit of womanhood!

Let's claim our rightful place, embrace our true essence, and forge ahead fearlessly, hand in hand, towards a brighter, harmonious tomorrow! But it is never too late to change your approach to finding happiness, understanding the specific changes needed, and acting.

It all begins with your expectations for the next phase of your Life. The more time you spend doing certain things one way, the more difficult it is to change your course as there will be resistance and avoidance. It is difficult to bluntly say that you have not been doing things the right way. It is not easy to say that you had to learn the hard way. It is not easy to start again.

And in the beginning, we all need some help. This book is about your success in re-launching your inner reflection and growth, leading to the best version of yourself.

Without growth, you cannot go past that frame of thought that has been constraining you for some time now. "As soon as you trust yourself, you will know how to live."- Johann Wolfgang von Goethe, Faust, First Part.

Reflecting on our past, we detach ourself logically and emotionally. When we embrace these odds that affect us mentally, there is resistance due to the judgment of oneself. It is okay to have a heavy heart. It is okay to admit we cannot do something independently and seek the help we need. No one knows what it feels like to be lonely until it becomes what we need.

There is an EQ (encephalization quotient) and IQ (intelligence quotient) regarding brain functionality. The EQ is responsible for our emotions. Any resistance is usually filtered through a negative rather than a positive lens. Our IQ is rational, which creates resistance, due to judgment and criticism.

To find our inner balance as human beings, we need to strike a balance between our rational vs. the emotional being, bringing us to harmony and ultimate contentment.

Unless we do so, we will never reach the ultimate point of harmony. I was not able to do it on my own. I was lucky enough to have different mentors (extremely wonderful and unbelievably bad), ultimately helping me understand, admit and move on from the past. And now, I am here to support your journey and pass my knowledge along.

But be aware. Nothing will ever happen by sitting and waiting for a miracle. Whatever you want and need - set goals and take each step, one at a time - day in and day out till you finally achieve them.

Deep down, I had to take many wrong turns to heal and become a healer, but it was not easy to admit my wrongs or even come to my senses in the first place. Ah, let me take you on a journey down the rabbit hole of my relapsed state. I found myself attracting a merry-go-round of people about as stable as a unicycle on a tightrope.

And to be completely honest, I wasn't the poster child for emotional stability either – we were all members of the "Emotional Rollercoaster Anonymous" club, riding the highs and lows like it was our full-time job!

It was like I had a magical magnet that drew in all the misfits, the emotional daredevils, and the drama enthusiasts. It was as if the universe was saying, "Hey, you there! Come one, come all – join the circus of emotional turmoil!"

Now, looking back, I can't help but chuckle at the cosmic comedy of it all. It was like we were all playing a chaotic game of emotional tag – each trying to outdo the other in a race to the bottom of the emotional barrel.

Picture this – we'd gather around the campfire of chaos, sharing stories of our emotional mishaps like it was a badge of honour. "You think you had a rough day? Ha! Let me tell you about the time I had three meltdowns before lunch!"

Now bring some eating and drinking into the equation and ask yourself: are you done with this BS? And boy, did we get good at playing the blame game. It was a masterclass in finger-pointing, with each of us pointing to the other and saying, "It's your fault I feel this way!" It was like a never-ending soap opera, and I had a front-row seat to the drama extravaganza.

But here's the kicker. I had an epiphany during all this chaos. It hit me like a ton of emotional bricks. Maybe, just maybe, I was contributing to this circus of emotional mayhem.

Yes, I had to face the truth that I wasn't exactly a pillar of emotional stability myself. Who needs stability when you can ride the emotional rollercoaster, right? It's like being on a never-ending thrill ride, with twists, turns, and loop-de-loops that leave you feeling exhilarated and slightly queasy.

But let me tell you, once I embraced the truth and decided to hop off the emotional rollercoaster, life took on a whole new flavour. It was like I had stepped into a world of emotional sanity where my feelings weren't pulling me in every direction like a tug-of-war match.

So, here's the takeaway, my fellow emotional daredevils – if you find yourself attracting a parade of emotionally unstable people, take a moment to look in the mirror and see if you're carrying an emotional "Welcome" sign. And if you are, it's time to flip that sign around and say, "Only emotionally stable folks allowed – drama enthusiasts need not apply. In fact, do me a favour and go f. yourself – I am not available!"

I'm not arguing that we ought to be emotional robots, utterly devoid of feelings. No, no, that would be no fun at all. Emotions are what make us beautifully and irrevocably human. But let's aim for a healthy dose of emotional stability and get ours together, like the perfect blend of salt and pepper on a scrumptious dish, and not necessarily pouring salt or pepper where it already bleeds…

So, buckle up, as the journey to emotional sanity may have a few bumps along the way, but trust me, it's worth every twist and turn. And who knows, maybe one day we'll look back and laugh at the emotional circus we once were and raise our glasses and have an actual bite at the emotionally stable, grounded, and gloriously hilarious beings we have become!

Ah, the marvellous journey of self-discovery and finding harmony is like navigating a maze of emotions and learning to juggle emotional grenades without blowing ourselves up! But fear not, for I have embarked on this wild adventure and intend to spice it up with a dash of humour and a pinch of sarcasm all the way – Life requires many ingredients to be worthwhile anyway. I and only I control my destiny. Now, about the law of attraction – it's like a cosmic magnet that draws in all the good, the bad, and the downright ugly. It's like having a superpower that attracts rainbows and thunderstorms! But here's the secret sauce – if you want to swim in a pool of positivity, you got to dive into the ocean of positive thoughts! It's like ordering a buffet of good vibes and leaving the negativity on the menu for someone else.

But let me tell you, being a compassionate soul is no easy feat. It's like having a superhero cape that magically absorbs everyone's troubles and transforms you into the Emotional Healer Extraordinaire!

And boy, do people love to dump their emotional baggage on you like it's a clearance sale! But hey, it's all part of the job – turning chaos into harmony is your superpower, and you rock it like a boss!

But here's the thing about blame – it's like playing a game of hot potato. Everyone wants to throw it at someone else, hoping to be rid of it for good. But guess what? The blame game is a never-ending carnival ride, and you realize you're stuck in a loop-de-loop of emotional turmoil sooner or later!

So, I decided to break free from this blame circus and unleash my inner predator! No, not the roaring kind with sharp teeth – I'm talking about becoming the hunter of my happiness. It's like saying, "Hey blame, you're not welcome here, so get lost!" And let me tell you, it's liberating!

And you know what's even better? Embracing the power of choice! It's like having a buffet of decisions, and you get to pick the ones that make your taste buds dance with delight! No more filling voids with empty relationships or empty jobs and empty bosses – now it's all about you choosing to add the right number of sprinkles of joy to your already fabulous life!

And let's not forget the importance of self-love – it's like the secret ingredient to a scrumptious life. You must sprinkle it on everything, like the fairy dust of happiness! Once you love yourself to the moon and back, you become a magnet for all things fabulous, like attracting a flock of unicorn admirers! How do you think kids make it all happen?

And you know what? It's time to let go of misery like a deflated balloon. Who needs it anyway? We've got a one-way ticket to the land of happiness, and we're leaving misery at the station! All aboard the Happiness Express!

So, here's the deal – thoughts become things, and the law of attraction works, only if you believe in your own magical powers. It's like having a genie in a bottle – you must rub that self-belief lamp and watch the magic unfold! Britney knows!

And guess what? Once that growth train starts chugging along, you'll feel like a superhero in steroids! You'll rock that with confidence, knowing that you've levelled up with every challenge. And here's the best part – you'll start seeing the awesomeness in yourself and others, like a sparkly disco ball illuminating the dance floor of life, like Cher does it!

So, my fellow journeyers, get on with it - strap on your capes, grab your magical wands of self-love and self-acceptance, and let's conquer this quest for harmony!

Let's create our own harmonic symphony and dance to the rhythm of our heartbeats – because when we realize our value and embrace the awesomeness within, the universe can't help but join the dance party of our dreams! Picture this. You'll be like a magnetic force of fabulousness, attracting your perfect match effortlessly. And we're not talking about just any path, oh no! We're talking about that special someone who takes your harmony to soaring heights!

It's like finding the missing piece to your puzzle, and boy, does it fit like a glove! Together, you'll create a symphony of love and joy, a duet of dreams and visions. Think two peas in a harmonious pod!

And hey, who knows, this cosmic duo might even come up with a secret handshake or a secret language only they can understand. I mean, it's all part of the cosmic fun! So, embrace your growth; own your worth, and get ready to attract the other half of your dynamic duo. You'll be unstoppable, unbreakable, and utterly indestructible together! Remember, life has an epic plan for you, and when you are in sync with your mission, the universe will give you high fives and fist bumps all the way! So, gear up for the adventure of a lifetime and get ready to dance to the rhythm of your purpose! Cosmic mission unlocked, darling!

Upon raising your consciousness, you'll unlock the hidden treasure trove of life's bounties. It's like stepping into a realm of endless possibilities and dazzling opportunities. You'll wonder why you ever settled for anything less!

Trust me, I've been there! Let me tell you a little secret. When I used to dwell on the negatives, it felt like being trapped in quicksand – the more I struggled, the deeper I sank. But when I finally unshackled myself from the chains of negativity, a new world of freedom opened before me!

The true essence of harmony lies in what you choose to embrace and what you decide to release – this is the law of attraction. Letting go of the burdensome baggage can liberate, like shedding the world's weight off your shoulders! So, why hold on to negativity? What does it bring you – more heartache, pain, joy, and happiness?

I say, it's time to hit the release button and let all those discouragements be fleeting moments in your journey. They are not here to prey on you but to awaken and propel you forward. It's all about growth and becoming stronger – a phoenix rising from the ashes!

And listen, let me make this crystal clear: no external person or situation can make you feel inferior without your consent. You are the gatekeeper of your worth, and once you recognize the value you truly deserve, the universe aligns to shower you with well-deserved successes! Remember, darling, you hold the pen to your life's story. You define yourself, you create your reality, and you set the stage for your own destiny. There are no limits to what you can achieve, for your thoughts and being are boundless! This is the law of attraction – period.

So, are you ready to take that daring leap of faith today? Write down your dreams, desires, and grand plans, and watch as the universe conspires to make them come true. In the words of George Bernard Shaw, "Life isn't about finding yourself; life is about creating yourself."

In my words, life is not about finding yourself - it's about unapologetically creating the extraordinary person you were born to be! So, let's throw open the curtains of creativity and paint your life with the most vibrant and dazzling colours! You've got this, my dear – seize the day with unbridled passion and embrace the unstoppable force that you are! Say hello to a boundless canvas of infinite possibilities where creativity knows no limits! Embrace a life painted with vibrant and dazzling colors, with each stroke crafting with the essence of your dreams and aspirations.

During your journey, remember that you hold the brush and the palette. Only you are the curator of your destiny, and the law of attraction will follow. With unbridled passion as your guide, seize the day and unleash the unstoppable force within you. Embrace the challenges, for they are the steppingstones toward your greatness. As you navigate through the symphony of opportunities, know that you are not alone.

I stand by your side, cheering you on, believing in your potential to create a profound impact. So, what are you waiting for? Embrace the call of innovation, fuel your spirit, and embark on this transformative journey.

With every stride you take, you'll rewrite the narrative of your life and leave an indelible mark on the world. It is not the time to paint a masterpiece that resonates with the depths of your soul. Embrace the challenge, and let your brilliance illuminate the path for others to follow. Your canvas awaits your touch, and the question echoes in your heart: What masterpiece will you create? Which colors will you choose? What legacy will you leave behind?

Unconditionally yours,
Vassilia

Printed in Great Britain
by Amazon

43333643R00069